*★*A BANTAM NATURE GUIDE*★*

KNOWLEDGE THROUGH COLOR

REPTILES OF THE WORLD

BY CARL GANS

A RIDGE PRESS BOOK/BANTAM BOOKS
TORONTO   NEW YORK   LONDON

Photo Credits

REPTILES OF THE WORLD

A Bantam Book published by arrangement with The Ridge Press, Inc.
Text prepared under the supervision of Laurence Urdang Inc.
Designed and produced by The Ridge Press, Inc. All rights reserved.
Copyright 1975 in all countries of the International Copyright Union
by The Ridge Press, Inc. This book may not be reproduced in whole or in part
by mimeograph or any other means, without permission. For information
address: The Ridge Press, Inc., 25 West 43rd Street, New York, N.Y. 10036.
Library of Congress Catalog Card Number: 74-19831
Published simultaneously in the United States and Canada.

Bantam Books are published by Bantam Books, Inc.
Its trademark, consisting of the words "Bantam Books" and the portrayal
of a bantam, is registered in the United States Patent Office
and in other countries. Marca Registrada.
Bantam Books, Inc., 666 Fifth Avenue, New York, N.Y. 10019
Printed in Italy by Mondadori Editore, Verona.

Contents

Introduction

What Are Reptiles?

The reptiles we see today represent the remnants of the group that engaged in the most successful adventure in history—the emergence from the waters in which animals originated and the invasion of dry land. Reptiles are not fishes, which tend to be aquatic animals that are clearly adapted to water. Nor are they amphibians, members of groups that evolved limbs and crawled away from the water only to remain tied to its vicinity by the aquatic habits of their young. Reptiles are clearly distinguished from fishes and amphibians by the development of the amniotic egg. This egg includes not only a hard outer shell, but also a set of internal membranes that enfold the growing embryo in a sheltered pool of amniotic fluid while the stored yolk is transformed into a baby snake or a turtle.

While reptiles are amniotes, so are birds and mammals. However, both of the latter clearly differ by their ability to maintain an elevated body temperature. Birds and mammals adjust their metabolic, or food utilization rate, to compensate for body heat lost. Reptiles cannot do this: they can only warm or cool their bodies by moving to a warmer or cooler spot of their environment. Thus turtles bask on a log and then cool off in the water when they get too hot. Consequently, reptiles may be defined as ectotherm amniotes.

Reptilian Adaptations

Reptiles are the group that first showed the major specializations that later made mammals successful. We must briefly treat these special adaptations in order to understand the reptilian success.

Temperature Regulation Most fish have the same temperature as the water in which they swim. They warm up somewhat when they swim faster: large fish have core temperatures higher than those of the surrounding waters. However, fish cool as they slow down and show little evidence of temperature control.

Reptiles have not yet developed a metabolic pattern that gives them
6 the scope (ability to increase metabolic rate) to maintain an elevated

Soft-shell Turtle

temperature. On the other hand, they have developed fairly accurate temperature sensors within their brains, and these steer their "ectothermal" behavior. Unless motivated by a conflicting drive, such as the activity of food objects or predators or the location of shelter sites, they will keep their body temperature very close to a preferred level that is maintained throughout the day's activity.

Metabolism Recent studies show that a running lizard uses about as much energy as a running mouse, squirrel, or chipmunk of the same weight running at the same speed. A snake sliding on its belly uses less (it is not carrying its weight off the ground), and swimming reptiles (or fish) use still less. Reptiles do have a lesser metabolic scope than do mammals. This limits the length of time that they can sustain running and foraging activities. Consequently, a lizard may dash as fast as a mouse but will rest thereafter to recover its energy store. The higher an animal's body temperature the greater its metabolic rate, but not necessarily its metabolic scope. The rate of oxygen transport (from air to lung to blood to cell) soon becomes limiting in reptiles.

Water Balance Reptiles need water for many purposes. If animals cannot drink, the concentration of salt in their blood, lymph, and tissue fluids increases and soon harms the cells. Reptiles sometimes use water to control their temperature: evaporation allows animals to pass heat to the outside air. While no reptile can sweat, some cool themselves by panting, but this generally indicates extreme temperature stress.

Water is also used to carry the waste products of metabolism through the kidneys. Fishes and amphibians flush their kidneys with enormous quantities of water. Life on dry land has caused reptiles to limit such wasteful usage. Excessive water loss has been controlled by transforming the skin into a barrier that will reduce evaporation and by developing an alternate mechanism for discharging metabolic wastes. The integumentary barrier is composed of a substance called keratin, first used for this purpose by amphibians but made much more effective in reptilian skin. The alternate mechanism for discharging metabolic **7**

Iguana

wastes involves the production of uric acid instead of ammonia or urea. A slight change in acidity causes this uric acid to crystallize in the cloaca, where the free water may then be resorbed to be used again. The urine of reptiles and many birds is a sludge of white crystals.

Reproduction Reptiles developed the amniotic egg, and all of their reproductive patterns reflect this specialization. Turtles, crocodilians, rhynchocephalians, and some squamates lay eggs. Many members of all three groups of squamates deposit the eggs only a few days before hatching or retain them until they are just about to hatch. Other forms retain the eggs until term, and the young are born alive.

In the latter case no outer shell is laid down. The soft outer membrane of the egg adheres closely to the wall of the oviduct of the mother. Wall and membrane are permeable to water and nutrients, which pass inward from the mother, and to waste products, which pass outward from the embryo. This permeable contact represents one of the earliest stages of placentation, parallel to the process later developed in mammals. In placental animals the egg's yolk contains only part of the raw materials required to form an embryo; the rest is provided by the mother between fertilization and birth.

Size and Growth Reptiles generally differ from mammals in having indeterminate growth. This means that they do not stop growing when they become sexually mature but continue to do so, though at a much slower rate, throughout the rest of their lives. Continuing growth, of course, makes it difficult to determine the maximum size achieved by a particular species. Consequently, a statement like "They tend to be about a foot long" refers to an average size, while "They grow up to 3 feet in length" refers to the maximum. Indeterminate growth also accounts for statements that some species of crocodilians or turtles are smaller than they used to be: hunting pressure on the population may have kept most specimens from becoming old enough to grow very large. Since the largest specimens tend to be most attractive to hide hunters, this is an obvious mechanism for reducing the average size.

Who Are the Reptiles?

The invasion of the land and the somewhat later invention of the amniotic egg opened up a whole new environment to the earliest reptiles. They could move into the drier areas, away from permanent water, and fossil records show an amazing diversity of forms that did so. We see many small species but also some truly spectacular large ones. Certainly dinosaurs are known to everyone. In the same way as such mammals as whales and seals later invaded the seas, so did the reptiles—as dolphin-like ichthyosaurs and turtle-like plesiosaurs. Bird-like pterosaurs flew—or at least glided—and may have approached endothermy, as some of them seem to have been covered with hair. We know that these various fossil reptiles fed on plants, on invertebrates, on fishes, and on each other. Once they were common; then, suddenly, during a relatively brief 5 million years, most of them became extinct for reasons that are still unclear and much debated.

Only six groups (orders) of the Class Reptilia survive today. Perhaps most primitive are the turtles, order Testudines, a group in which the shoulder and pelvic girdles have moved to the inside of a bony shell and achieved a curious box-like construction, unique among the vertebrates. Turtles, which bury their eggs in the soil and neither guard them nor practice parental care, occur in a wide belt throughout the temperate and tropical zones.

There are 20 species of the order Crocodilia, which derive from a line of reptiles that later gave rise to birds. They are relatively large aquatic animals that range around the tropical and subtropical parts of the world. Some species exceeded 20 feet in length, though such enormous beasts are now rare. Surviving crocodilians are probably insignificant relatives of some now-extinct forms that apparently reached lengths of 60 feet or so. All species that evolved during the Recent epoch are egg-layers and carnivores, and even the smallest species exceeds 3 feet in length.

Next there is the order Rhynchocephalia or beak-nosed reptiles. A single living species, the Tuatara, survives precariously on a few islands **9**

King Cobra

off New Zealand, most members of the order having become extinct long ago.

Finally, we come to the superorder Squamata or scaly reptiles that includes the largest number of the successful groups living today. The superorder Squamata includes three orders—amphisbaenians, lizards, and snakes. Rigid definitions of such groups tend to become technical, but amphisbaenians (formerly called worm-lizards) are slender reptiles with a thin, flexible, and annulate (ringed) skin subdivided into squarish segments. The head is specialized for ramming and forming tunnels, and the ear for hearing prey while underground. Some 130 species of the order Amphisbaenia range from Patagonia to Florida in the New World and from South Africa to Spain, Turkey, and Iran in the Old.

The approximately 3,100 lizards (order Sauria) include a bewildering array of species. More than 20 families are currently recognized. Most species have limbs and a more or less elongate tail; they are covered with a scaly skin studded with "scales" which are tuberculate—flattened or conical projections of keratin. They range from the Arctic circle (in Europe) to the southern tips of South America, Africa, and India, as well as across Australia and New Zealand.

Snakes (order Ophidia) seem to be a more recent development, and the approximately 2,300 species are apparently the group of reptiles most successful today. Except for their absence from oceanic islands, they have a distribution approximately equivalent to that of lizards. However, the marine sea snakes extend this range, for they occur across vast regions of the Indian and Pacific Oceans. Snakes are always limbless, though a few species retain remnants of the pelvic girdle. Head and jaws are highly mobile, and most snakes move the two halves of the lower jaw separately by alternating left and right grasping pulls while ingesting their food. They characteristically swallow their prey whole, stretching around large food items.

Within this general body plan we see an amazing array of specializations. For example, some snakes have specialized for a single food item

Tuatara

such as bird eggs, the soft portions of snails, fish eggs, and centipedes.

Understanding and Study

Much has been learned about reptiles. Some of the diverse aspects of our interest are stated here. Other subjects will be introduced in the following accounts. Actually, however, we do not yet know very much even about the numbers and kinds of reptiles, particularly of those found in tropical regions. Some species are likely to become extinct before we have discovered that they exist. Their discovery and description are an international undertaking, and the Latin names of families given in the Table of Contents and of species in the text serve as an international index to the facts which we have thus far discovered.

As we begin to know Who the many reptiles are, we can ask more significant questions, such as How do they utilize their environment? How much of their energy do they obtain from the plants and animals upon which they feed and how much directly from the sun by basking? The many curious reptilian activities are not randomly assembled, charming facts in natural history: instead they are strategies for survival and success under sometimes quite inhospitable circumstances. The questions become even more interesting when we ask how numerous reptiles can live in one area. How do they divide up the resources? Why is it possible for 20 kinds to survive in one place and only a dozen in another?

Seen from this viewpoint, every change in anatomy or structure, in physiology, and in behavior may reflect an adaptation to local circumstances. The understanding of reptiles then leads to an improved understanding about the ways all animals interact with each other and with their physical environment.

Some reptiles may be appreciated for their intrinsic beauty. A look from the basis of their complex specialization teaches us to appreciate even more the intricate web of interlocking specializations. Now that we have a general idea of reptiles, let us look at individuals. **11**

Turtles

Common Snapping Turtle
Chelydra serpentina

The Common Snapping Turtle is one of two species of a genus that ranges across North America, from southeastern Alberta to Texas, and continues west to New Mexico and south through Central America to Ecuador. Snappers have a shell length of up to 19 inches and may reach a weight of more than 28 pounds.

In contrast to the Alligator Snapper, this aquatic species is a good swimmer and an active predator. While it will take carrion, it subsists on practically all aquatic animals as well as many kinds of water plants. This omnivorous habit probably accounts for some of the animal's success, as does its ability to move freely on land, a walk of more than five miles having been recorded. Walking may be facilitated by the ventrally wide-open shell, which allows the legs more freedom of movement than in many other turtles. Snappers tend to be much more aggressive when surprised on land than when they are approached in the water.

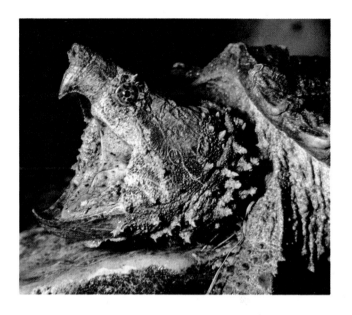

Alligator Snapping Turtle

Macroclemys temminckii

The Alligator Snapping Turtle of the southeastern United States is the largest North American freshwater turtle, the record specimen weighing 236 pounds. These turtles live about 60 years. They are primarily bottom walkers, rather than swimmers, in the slowly moving waters where they live, even though they do have to stretch their necks to the surface to take in air. The shell is folded into three ridges, has jagged edges, and is quite rough. It tends to be covered with algae, helping to camouflage the animal.

This snapper's feeding method is most peculiar. He has a long, loose protuberance at the end of his tongue: this process may be filled with blood, which colors it red; when wiggled, it resembles a moving worm. The hapless fish that swims into the open mouth to grab this ''worm'' is caught between the turtle's closing jaws.

Stinkpot

Sternotherus odoratus

This high-domed musk turtle ranges over the eastern half of the United States and is often observed fleetingly in ponds and lakes by fishermen and swimmers. It is the most common member of a group of three musk and five mud turtles in the United States. Most of the other species have much smaller ranges, mostly in the southeastern United States, with some found in the southwestern states and Mexico.

The pointed snout of the musk turtle is always recognizable by the two white lines forming an angle on each side. The plastron has two prominent hinges so that the shell can be closed tightly when the animal is disturbed. The name Stinkpot derives from the pungent secretion produced by glands at the margin of the shell and expelled when the turtle is removed from the water.

Central American River Turtle
Dermatemys mawii

This large river turtle, which exceeds 2 feet in shell length, is found on the eastern side of Central America, in a region extending from southern Mexico to Guatemala and Honduras. It is a thoroughly aquatic species, so much so that it is said to have trouble moving on land or even holding its head clear of the ground for any length of time. Adult females lay about 20 eggs which they cover with decaying vegetation. Otters prey specifically on members of this species.

This large river turtle is of considerable interest to the specialist because it represents the only surviving member of a family that might have been intermediate between the mud and the pond turtles and might have given rise to the latter family.

Big-headed Turtle

Platysternon megacephalum

The southeast Asian Big-headed Turtle appears disproportionate, as if head and tail have outgrown the shell. The skull is enormous and cannot be withdrawn beneath the shell, which is normally about 5 to 6 inches long, although the total length of the turtle is about 12 inches. The top of the head is armored, which provides it with some protection.

The species lays only two eggs at a time, and is supposed to feed largely upon invertebrates; when disturbed, it emits a squeaking call.

A fast swimmer and an excellent climber, the Big-headed Turtle occurs through a wide range of southeast Asia, from Burma to China, in lowlands and in mountain streams.

Spotted Turtle
Clemmys guttata

The Spotted Turtle is one of the prettiest of North American turtles. Specimens are easily recognized by the series of bright-yellow spots scattered across the blue-black background of its shell. The ventral surface is yellow to orange and has black blotches along the outer edges.

Spotted Turtles favor marshy areas and are omnivorous, capturing food on land and in the water. They prefer cooler temperatures than many other turtles and have been observed mating at 10°C (50°F).

Though it ranges from extreme northern Illinois east to Massachusetts and in a narrow belt south along the coastal states to Georgia, the Spotted Turtle is not common anywhere. **17**

Wood Turtle

Clemmys insculpta

The Wood Turtle is a beautiful and apparently quite intelligent pond turtle that was once quite common in the central and northeastern United States. Individuals ranged widely over the forested areas feeding on plants, small invertebrates, and occasionally on carrion.

The shell is irregular and has a series of sculptured ridges rising to the center of each scale of the carapace. Wood Turtles mate underwater and lay from four to 12, generally about seven or eight, eggs. These turtles hear quite well and learn to run mazes about as well as rats do. They are now protected in several of the eastern United States.

Indian Snail-eating Turtle

Malayemys trijuga

This medium-sized species is found in several rivers of the northern portion of the Indian peninsula. It is a true pond turtle, being highly aquatic and coming to shore only to bask or to lay eggs.

They feed on aquatic snails, which they recognize by sight or smell and peel out of their shell before swallowing. To do this the turtle first crushes the snail, then alternately distends and constricts its throat, flushing water into and out of the mouth. This washes the fragments of broken shell away from the soft parts, which are held loosely by the ridges of the half-opened jaws and swallowed when clean.

The juveniles are particularly attractive because of the clear yellow bands along the sides of the snout.

▲ *Malayemys trijuga* ▼ A sub-species

Terrapin or Slider

Chrysemys scripta

The Slider turtles occur across the Americas from the United States south to Argentina. Most Terrapins are medium-sized, greenish animals with patterns of yellow, green, and sometimes red lines radiating along the sides of the head. They are the pond and river turtles that one often sees basking on logs and stumps along rivers, ponds, and irrigation canals. The basking probably helps them to dry out and control the aquatic parasites that attach to the shell and lets them utilize the ultraviolet light from the sun to produce compounds necessary for bone deposition. Equally important, these turtles thus can raise their body temperature to a level at which digestion and other processes proceed more efficiently.

Young Terrapins are often very pretty and, consequently, nests are robbed all over the range and the hatchlings sold as living toys. Deplorably, most such pets die of food deficiencies long before they mature.

Common Box Turtle

Terrapene carolina

The North American Box Turtles look like tortoises and are most closely related to pond turtles. The carapace is high-domed and the plastron is beautifully hinged. The shell may close so tightly that not even a blade of grass can be inserted.

The group ranges across the eastern and central United States into northern Mexico and is quite common in certain areas. Its survival over this wide but only partially occupied zone may reflect such reptilian specialization as sperm storage, which permits successful reproduction at very low population densities: females may produce several clutches of eggs after only a single mating. There is little question that specimens live to be 100 years old and females are supposed to be still capable of producing offspring at 50.

Gopher Tortoise
Gopherus polyphemus

Various Gopher Tortoises of the southern United States are the only true tortoises of North America. They dig long, underground retreats by shoveling the soil with their forefeet and then pushing the loosened dirt out of the entrance. Burrows have been traced for over 40 feet and with the deepest part 10 feet underground. These tunnels are remarkable structures when one bears in mind that the turtle is only about a foot long. Many other animals share these tunnel systems.

The two species of these medium-sized animals feed mainly on plant material. The Western Desert Tortoise subsists mainly on cactus from which it extracts the water, allowing it to inhabit regions where there are few opportunities for drinking. Gopher Tortoises are endangered and are now protected.

Jaboty or Forest Tortoise

Geochelone denticulata

Two large tortoises range over the forest and savanna regions of northern and central South America east of the Andes. Until recently the two were confused, but it is now clear that the smaller Red-footed Tortoise occupies mostly the open savannas while the larger Jaboty (here illustrated) occupies forest localities. Interestingly enough, when confined in gardens the forest form will not bask in the sun, but hides in the shade of low vegetation.

The name Red-footed reflects the fact that young specimens have the scales of head and limbs colored a bright orange, which gradually becomes obscured as they mature.

The forest form reaches a maximum shell length of 27 inches in eastern Peru, though specimens in other parts of the range are little more than a foot long.

Galápagos Giant Tortoise

Geochelone elephantopus

The isolated volcanic islets of the Galápagos archipelago, some 200 miles from the coast of Ecuador, are inhabited by a group of giant tortoises that were made famous during Darwin's exploration of these islands. Specimens with shells 5 feet long and almost 3 feet in height were once common, and these weighed well over 450 pounds.

It is remarkable that the tortoises of islands only 30 miles apart show such different and characteristic shell shapes that local hunters could identify the islands from which they had been collected. This immediately raised questions regarding the origin of such variation. Populations now on islands where vegetation grows higher seem to be saddle-backed: the shell is bent upward at the neck so that they can browse. The grass-eaters have a more characteristic domed shell.

These tortoises are coadapted to the other life on these islands, for the seeds of some local plants will germinate much more readily if they have first passed through the gut of a giant tortoise.

Aldabra Giant Tortoise

Geochelone gigantea

Aldabra Giant Tortoises once occupied all of the Seychelles archipelago in the Indian Ocean; now they remain only on the island of Aldabra where they are quite common. These tortoises represent another case of giant animals on isolated oceanic islands that achieved their size in the absence of predators. The Aldabra Giant Tortoise also used to be hunted for food and oil: the living turtles were used by pirates, merchantmen, and whalers as a fresh meat supply on long voyages.

On Aldabra, the tortoises breed in the spring, the male emitting a roaring sound as it pursues the female. There are good records of specimens living well over 150 years, but most of the growth takes place during the first 25.

▲ Galápagos Giant Tortoise ▼ Aldabra Giant Tortoise

Leopard Tortoise

Geochelone pardalis

This large tortoise reaches a shell length of almost 2 feet and occurs over the vast savanna areas of Africa and up into the lower mountains. They are beautiful animals with a high, domed carapace; each scale of the back is marked with an irregular pattern of black and yellow. India and Africa show several related species of tortoise in which the coloration is more geometrically regular. For instance, the Star Tortoise of India shows a radiating series of yellow lines on each dark-brown scale.

Leopard Tortoises feed almost exclusively on grasses and the fruit of low-lying bushes. The shell is very stout and provides some protection from larger predators, although not from man. The size of wild populations may well be limited by periodic grass fires, which they can escape only if a river is nearby or when they can enter a burrow.

Pancake Tortoise
Malacochersus tornieri

The medium-sized (shell length 8 inches) Pancake Tortoise occurs in a few areas of eastern Africa where it browses on the vegetation of the open, rocky plains. The legs are very long and the turtles are very active: not only are they able to right themselves quickly when placed on their backs, but they can also run across open areas at a speed almost twice that of ordinary tortoises.

The shell feels soft because the bone normally underlying the carapace is only laid down as an outline, leaving large windows along the sides of the back, a unique condition among land turtles. When these animals were first discovered it was assumed that specimens with this many holes in the bony armor must be diseased; later books suggested, in error, that these tortoises could blow themselves up to resist being pulled out of the rocky cracks in which they rested at night. Actually, they depend upon speed rather than armor for escape from their predators, for the holes in the shell make for a lighter-weight animal that can run faster and longer.

Greek Tortoise
Testudo graeca

This is one of several Mediterranean tortoises or land turtles whose range extends from northern Africa across Asia Minor into Iran and southern Russia. They have long been kept as pets in northern Europe.

These are tortoises with a thick, hard, unhinged shell, attractively marked with various designs of browns, tans, and white. The two openings in the shell are blocked by folding the limbs inward; the projecting portions of the animal bear thick spines of bone and keratin.

Such turtles are called tortoises in Europe while many of the semi-aquatic species are referred to as terrapins there. Unfortunately, there **28** are fewer common names than there are groups of turtles.

▲ Newly hatched Loggerhead ▼ Adult

Loggerhead Turtle

Caretta caretta

This turtle occurs in the Atlantic and also has an extensive range throughout the Indian Ocean and the Pacific. It is still believed that Atlantic and Pacific Loggerheads belong to the same species. The name comes from its enormous head, which is nearly twice as wide as that of the green turtle and apparently well fitted for feeding on bottom-dwelling invertebrates such as sea urchins and giant starfish.

Like all other sea turtles the Loggerheads lay their eggs on selected beaches in specific seasons. Dozens or hundreds of animals may come ashore in a restricted area during a relatively short period of time. They dig holes with their hind flippers and deposit between 100 and 350 eggs 5 to 22 inches deep in the sand. After covering over the nest, the mother roughs up the surface of the beach over a wide area in order to hide the exact nesting place. The young all hatch at the same time. As they start to scramble upward simultaneously, they break down the roofing soil and continue moving on it as it falls. Escape from the nest is thus a communal affair; hatchlings from individual eggs buried beneath 20 inches of sand would probably perish. **29**

Green Turtle

Chelonia mydas

Green Turtles, specimens of which weigh up to 300 pounds, used to inhabit the Atlantic Ocean from southern Canada south to Argentina. The Pacific Green Turtle belongs to a different species. The Green Turtle used to be an important food resource of the people inhabiting shores and islands of the Atlantic coast. The flesh is delicious, the shell forms the basis for a soup, and the eggs are a staple item in many Latin American countries.

Green Turtles feed on marine algae and migrate from great distances in a pattern that is only now being studied by marking specimens as they come to nest on the breeding beaches of Central America and trailing animals taken in other areas. If the animals were protected on the breeding sites and allowed to recover from the wholesale hunting to which they have been exposed, they could continue to provide an important food resource for tropical areas.

Hawksbill Turtle
Eretmochelys imbricata

The thin layer of horny keratin that covers the shell of most turtles is very much thickened in the Hawksbill Turtle and shows a beautiful yellow-brown translucence when peeled from the shell. This modification of the relatively small (200-pound) sea turtle is the valuable tortoise shell, once used for luxury combs, boxes, and jewelry. Such objects are now made from plastics, fortunately, as the scales were once peeled off the living animal with boiling water and the turtle released to grow another layer.

Like all sea turtles the Hawksbill propels itself with its front flippers. These act as a pair of hydrofoils and exert forward forces both during the upstroke and the downstroke, the hind feet being used primarily for steering. Like all other turtles, the Hawksbill uses the hind feet to excavate the nest.

This species occurs in several races across much of the Atlantic and Pacific Oceans. **31**

Leatherback Turtle or Luth

Dermochelys coriacea

The Leatherback or Luth is the largest living turtle: it grows to more than 1,400 pounds in weight and may have a shell length of about 6 feet. Curiously, it also has the widest range of any reptile. Its role among sea turtles has been compared to that of the giant albatross among sea birds: both range far over tropical and temperate oceans. Leatherbacks have been caught off Australia and near the northern tip of Norway, and a recent monograph was based on a specimen that had managed to end up in the Baltic.

These large turtles lack an outer horny covering to the shell, and even its inner support is provided only by a loose series of small bones rather than solid, interlocking plastron and carapace. The neck contains a heavy sheathing of fat and cannot be retracted within the shell.

Leatherbacks seem to feed on large marine invertebrates, mainly on big jellyfish, including the Portuguese man-of-war, the sting of which is very dangerous to man. Perhaps the heavy, horny papillae lining its throat protect the turtle.

Indian Soft-shelled Turtle
Chitra indica

This curiously small-headed, soft-shelled turtle is clearly the largest species of its group. Annandale claimed that its shell approaches 6 feet in length and that the turtle was capable of attacking and sinking small boats (though presumably not doing much harm to the occupants).

The brown shell is, at least in smaller specimens, marked with wavy lines, while the sides of the head are striped. The most astonishing aspect of the animal is the extremely small head. The skull seems even smaller than it really is because the eyes and nostrils are crammed onto its anteriormost portion. Clearly the animal is highly adapted for life in muddy rivers. Like some submarines, only the "periscope" and air intake need be exposed to aerial predators.

The species lives in the large rivers of the Indian peninsula from Pakistan to Malaysia.

Nile Soft-shelled Turtle

Trionyx triunguis

The Nile Soft-shell is a member of an unusual group that retains only a loose framework of internal connecting bones within the shell: the outside plates or scales have become completely lost, hence the name.

Soft-shelled turtles are excellent swimmers, and various species range over the rivers and lakes of the North American continent while others, such as the species illustrated, are found in Africa, along the Mediterranean, and through southern Asia. Their flattened bodies excellently adapt these animals to life on the bottoms of water courses. They often hide in shallow mud and sand banks, breathing by extending their long neck to the surface with only the snorkel-like nasal tips and possibly the protuberant eyes emerging when they take a breath. Most soft-shells are very effective predators, and the head shoots forth to grab the prey.

These animals can exchange some gases via their cloaca, which makes them susceptible to some of the respiratory poisons used to remove "trash fish" from rivers and reservoirs.

New Guinean Plateless Turtle

Carettochelys insculpta

Although the plateless turtle superficially resembles the soft-shelled turtles, this animal represents a completely different family of which it seems to be the only surviving species. Its shell is only 18 inches long and lacks even traces of horny shields. The front flippers have almost lost their toes and become paddle-shaped. Here, again, an animal's external appearance is not enough to tell us what the closest relative might be. Differences of the internal bones of the shell (missing in true soft-shells) suggest that it may be intermediate between the crypto-diran and the side-necked (pleurodiran) turtles.

The species is unique among freshwater turtles in that it swims mainly with the forefeet, which have been developed into hydrofoils like those of marine turtles, adapting it well for the rivers of New Guinea.

Arrau Turtle

Podocnemis expansa

The Arrau is the largest of the South American turtles. Like the Mata-mata, it is a side-necked turtle that withdraws its head by bending it laterally under the margin of the shell.

Once these turtles occurred in enormous numbers in the Orinoco and Amazon river systems where they reached up to 150 pounds with shell lengths of 35 inches. Stories abound of nesting migrations to sand banks along the river where thousands of turtles deposited 80 to 200 eggs each. Such occasional mass abundance, first of eggs and then of almost defenseless hatchling turtles, apparently exceeds the predatory capacities of the local birds and mammals so that enough turtles survive to scatter to smaller tributaries where they grow to maturity.

African Mud Turtle

Pelusios subniger

This is one of some half-dozen side-necked turtles of Africa, the classification of which is still confused. Since this turtle resembles many other aquatic turtles in the drastic changes in its body proportions and coloration during growth, it is difficult to identify the several forms. Consequently, it will be some time before we know how many species there actually are in this genus.

The present species supposedly ranges from Senegal in extreme Western Africa across the continent to the island of Zanzibar and even to Madagascar. These small to medium-sized turtles (shell length 11½ inches) are found in streams and permanent ponds, as well as in the pans or seasonal waterholes that promote game concentration in the high plains country. They are good swimmers and omnivorous, predating and scavenging. **37**

▲ Close-up, *Chelodina longicollis* ▲ River Terekay ▼ Snorkeling—*Chelodina expansa*

River Terekay
Podocnemis unifilis

This smaller relative of the Arrau rarely reaches 8 inches in length. It is a pretty turtle, characterized by bright-yellow markings on the sides of the face.

Besides stalking the small invertebrates and fishes which compose much of its prey, this river turtle has developed the curious habit of skimming the surface of the water for the film of small plants and invertebrates that forms in late summer on some of the oxbows where it makes its home. To do this it opens its mouth wide and distends the throat to make a deep pocket. It then drops the head until a thin sheet of water just passes the edge of the lower jaw. The surface tension then pulls floating materials across this weir. As soon as the throat is full the Terekay closes the mouth, blows the water out through the nostrils, and swallows the nutritious remnants.

Snake-necked River Turtle
Chelodina longicollis

Pleurodires, or side-necked turtles, are found mainly in the southern continents, Africa, South America, and Australia. Their distribution may reflect the drifting of continents, and some workers suspect that they may have reached their present homes by passing over Antarctica, before that continent was covered with ice. Two major groups, the short-necked and the long-necked pleurodires, occur in Australia.

One representative of the long-necked pleurodires occurring in Australia is this common Snake-necked Turtle that lives in the swamps and marshes, rather than rivers and lakes, of eastern Australia. Like many aquatic turtles it feeds mostly on animal food, taking small fishes, small frogs, shrimp, and snails. The long neck allows the turtle to dart forth at prey; equally important, it allows the turtle to breathe by snorkeling: resting on the bottom, the turtle can stretch its neck to the surface and withdraw it again without having to leave its hiding place or swim upward.

Mata-mata Turtle

Chelus fimbriatus

The Mata-mata Turtle of the streams of northern South America has restructured itself into an elegant fishtrap. When a growth of algae covers the shell it is almost impossible to recognize the turtle hiding at the river bottom. Each scale of the shell rises to a peak and the edge of the shell is jagged. The skin of the limbs and head is covered with loose flaps, folds, and fringes that float with water currents. The name "Mata-mata," which means "loose skin" in an Indian dialect, is perfectly chosen. The head is pointed and the eyes small, protected, and camouflaged. The mouth is wide and the throat enormous. When hunting, the Mata-mata tenses the throat muscles and then suddenly releases a ratchet on the mouth, causing it to spring open, allowing an inrush of water that sweeps small fishes into the throat. Several little flaps of skin near the edge of the mouth detect the movements of passing fishes, and the trap is triggered more by touch than by sight.

Crocodilians

American Alligator
Alligator mississippiensis

The American Alligator and its close relative, the Chinese Alligator, found only in the Yangtze Valley, are remnants of one of two major groups of crocodilians. They are certainly the only crocodilians now confined entirely to temperate regions. American Alligators were once common in the estuaries and river courses of the coastal regions from North Carolina to Texas. Recently their range has been reduced, and they are now protected over its entire area.

As with other crocodilians, the juvenile period is the most critical time for the alligator. After burying some 50 or more eggs in a mixture of rotting vegetation, the female stays close and defends the general nesting area until the young hatch.

These animals are known to reach lengths of 18 to 19 feet, although records of such size are rare.

Spectacled Caiman

Caiman crocodilus

Of the five species of caiman that inhabit South and Central America, the Spectacled Caiman is the most widely distributed. These forms used to be extremely common in the Amazon and other large water courses in South America, where populations have been recently decimated by hunting.

Relatively little is known about their feeding habits: as far as reported, they mainly subsist on fishes but will take other small animals as available. There is good indication that small Caimans are occasionally taken by the Anaconda, a large aquatic snake. Healthy adult animals are ordinarily not bothered by Piranha even though they often share the same water courses.

Recent records average slightly more than 6 feet in length, but earlier records suggest that specimens used to grow larger.

Nile Crocodile

Crocodylus niloticus

This is the second largest of the crocodilians, reaching approximately 19 feet and weighing 2,000 pounds. These effective predators once occupied a range from the vicinity of the Cape of Good Hope, across much of Africa, and down the Nile Valley into the Mediterranean. Today they are restricted to populations in isolated preserves.

The males apparently have breeding territories, and the females deposit and bury a hundred or so eggs above the high-water line on sand banks of shorelines. The young call when they hatch and the female digs open the nest, picks them up in her mouth, and carries the hatchlings singly or in pairs to the water.

Adult males have been known to attack motorboats, apparently mistaking the sound of the outboard for the signal of a competing male. **43**

Mugger

Crocodylus palustris

The Mugger, the most snub-nosed of the crocodiles, ranges all across the Indian peninsula and Burma, crossing the open ocean to reach Sri Lanka (Ceylon). The animals were formerly revered, and there are a number of temples in which large specimens are still kept and regularly fed offerings. Like most other crocodilians, this species is probably endangered, but we know very little about the number that currently survives.

The Mugger belongs to those crocodilians, like the Gavial and most other large crocodiles, that hide their eggs in a sand or gravel bank adjacent to the water. In contrast, some of the smaller species, as well as the American Alligator and, curiously enough, the saltwater crocodile, embed their eggs in a mass of rotting vegetation, which they collect and assemble adjacent to the water.

Estuarine Crocodile

Crocodylus porosus

This is the largest of crocodilians. These estuarine animals have been documented at lengths over 20 feet with weights well over a ton. While the species ranges from Sri Lanka (Ceylon) to Australia, the largest specimens appear to have been taken in the Philippines, mostly at the end of the last and the beginning of the present century. Many crocodiles enter the coastal zones of the oceans, but the Estuarine Crocodile regularly swims far out to sea, and its distribution suggests that specimens have traveled more than a hundred miles of open ocean.

While the species subsists mainly on fish, it will attack other large animals, and in former times there were many records of attacks on man.

West African Dwarf Crocodile

Osteolaemus tetraspis

Western Africa is the home of three kinds of crocodiles: the Nile Crocodile, which once ranged from the Cape to the Mediterranean; the Armored Crocodile, restricted to the rivers and the great lakes of Western and Central Africa; and the West African Dwarf Crocodile, isolated in the smaller rivers and ponds.

Two separate populations of short-snouted dwarf crocodiles occur: that of the extreme West African forests is characterized by an anteriorly bent snout, while that from northeastern Zaire has a more nearly straight snout. Although the maximum size of modern crocodiles ranges from 20 to 25 feet in length, the adult dwarf crocodile is less than 6 feet long.

It would be interesting to know how these small animals compete with juvenile specimens of the Nile Crocodile, which are known for their propensity for walking long distances up river courses and which may, therefore, occasionally coexist with this short-snouted species.

Gavial or Gharial

Gavialis gangeticus

The Gavial or Gharial is a large and specialized crocodile once occupying the great rivers of India, Pakistan, and Upper Burma, but now having a more spotty range. These slender animals exceed 19 feet in length, being one of the longest of the reptiles. Some fossil species, known mainly from skulls, must have been almost 60 feet long.

In males the tip of the elongate snout is capped by a balloon-like nasal flap. The snout is extremely narrow and consists of little more than four rows of interlocking teeth (two upper and two lower) and an armored air passage. It serves as an efficient fishtrap when utilized for sideways snaps at schools of fish. Once caught by the tip of the jaws, a fish is likely to be tossed into the air, being moved backward with each toss until it disappears headfirst down the Gavial's throat.

Beak-Heads

Tuatara
Sphenodon punctatus

These unusual animals resemble 2-foot-long lizards. Actually they are remnants of a group of reptiles that was once thought to have become extinct 200 million years ago. Since their rediscovery 140 years ago, they have been studied intensively, but new curiosities are regularly uncovered. Tuataras differ from lizards, among other ways, by having two rather than one bony arcade framing the back of the skull. Curiously, their preferred temperature is about 13°C (56°F)—more than 10° less than that preferred by any other reptile of the Recent epoch.

Their hatchlings resemble turtles, crocodilians, and birds in having a caruncle, or keratinous bump, on the nose with which they break the eggshell from the inside. Eight to 14 eggs laid at a time must be incubated for 13 to 14 months; the animals are known to live more than 77 years, much longer than recorded for any lizard or snake.

The species is restricted to a few rocky islands off the coast of New Zealand where the remnant population is strictly protected.

Amphisbaenians

White Amphisbaena
Amphisbaena alba

This is probably the largest of all the amphisbaenians. Specimens grow to more than 2 feet in length and almost an inch and a half in diameter. This formidable predator lives underground in a variety of forest and plains localities across the South American continent east of the Andes, from Panama to Paraguay.

It moves by sliding its loose, sleeve-like skin forward then backward over the body: portions of the skin are pressed to the ground and the body is then pulled forward from these. Its jaws are relatively large and upper and lower teeth interlock, letting the animal crush the shells of beetles and the bones of lizards and small mammals. Like all other species of its order, the White Amphisbaena tracks its prey by sound: the sensitive zone has shifted from the back of the head to the side of the lower jaw, which is connected by a cartilaginous amplifying rod directly to the middle ear.

There are many reports on the association of this species with the nests of leaf-cutting ants, but we know next to nothing of how they manage to avoid the soldiers defending these.

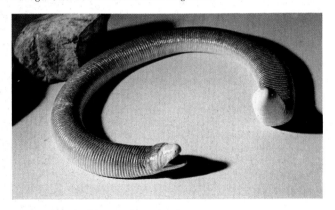

South African Shield-snouted Amphisbaenian
Monopeltis capensis

This is a member of one of the more specialized amphisbaenian lines. The facial portion of the snout has become spade-shaped with the face covered by some soft tissues then again enfolded in a heavy layer of keratin. This arrangement represents high modification for tunneling. The snout is first rammed into the tunnel's end, up to the level of the eye. The *Monopeltis* then rotates the head upward compressing the soil into the roof of the tunnel. The need to exert pressure on the wall of the tunnel has not only resulted in the stiffening of the shield but has also forced the jaws to be reduced. The number of teeth is less than in the round-headed White Amphisbaena and the eyes have become smaller and have been displaced to the sides.

Members of this group grow up to 2 feet in length and lay their eggs mostly in the large termite hills found on the high plains of southern Africa. Other species of the genus range from the Cameroons to South Africa and to Tanzania. This South African species ranges from the Cape Province north to the southern borders of Zambia and into Mozambique and Angola.

Two-legged Amphisbaenian
Bipes biporus

The members of this family (Bipedidae) are unique among amphisbaenians in having retained the shoulder girdle and very functional hands. These forelimbs lie far forward on the body and are so incongruous that the animal has been called "Lagartija con oreillas" or "little lizard with big ears." They appear to be bright pink, but the color is actually produced by the blood which shines through the translucent skin.

They dig underground burrows and apparently use their forelegs only for making the first entry into the soil and for widening tunnel chambers underground, then flattening them against the body for regular tunneling. The forelegs can fold almost 180° at each joint and may consequently be brought forward alongside the body even in a very narrow tunnel.

The three known species inhabit different parts of Mexico, with the two-pored species shown restricted to the tip of Baja California.

▲ Overall view and close-up of South African shield-snout

Two views of the "little lizard with big ears"

Somali Edge-snouted Amphisbaenian

Agamodon anguliceps

The Somali Edge-snouted Amphisbaenian is one of some half-dozen members of a family (Trogonophidae) placed together because their teeth are fused as bumps on the edge of the bony jaw rather than in sockets against the jaw's edge. These species occupy the deserts from Morocco to Tunisia and from Iran across Saudi Arabia to Socotra Island and Somalia.

They have become specialized for tunneling in sand by an oscillating movement in which the body alternately rotates left and right. The Somali species has a triangular rather than circular cross-section of the body, a shortening of the trunk, and a downward curved, pointed tail. All of these features keep the trunk stable when the animal moves.

The beautiful and protective blotched coloration is similar to that of the surface sand of the deserts they inhabit. An example is given by this **52** species from Somalia which is about 4 inches long.

Lizards

Mexican Snake Lizard
Anelytropsis papillosus

Some tropical parts of the world are inhabited by isolated animals, the affinities of which leave us thoroughly confused. Examples are the three species of the genus *Dibamus* from New Guinea and a few Indo-Malaysian islands, and this rare snake lizard from Mexico of which only some dozen specimens have thus far been found. All of these lizards have a skull reduced for burrowing, are almost blind, and lack limbs. The skin is covered with scales, like those of snakes. Few people have seen either Snake Lizard alive; some experts believe them to be most closely related to the skinks while others say that they form a missing link "between lizards and snakes." Recent studies on their brains suggest that the Mexican animals are indeed most closely related to those of New Guinea. Such a curious situation certainly deserves a bit more investigation.

Tokay
Gekko gecko

The east Asiatic Tokay is one of the larger members of the gecko family. Like many other geckos it can walk on walls and even on the ceiling. The scales beneath the toes are covered with cells that send out fine, hair-like processes that adhere to a surface when pressed into contact with it. The Tokay's large mouth and sharp teeth make it an excellent predator.

Like some other tree geckos, it has taken to sharing human habitation and may often be seen around lights picking up the insects attracted to them. Even large roaches, mantids, and beetles, as well as small vertebrates are taken. Most geckos are nocturnal and their eyes are well adapted for night vision.

Geckos produce sounds and apparently hear well. They are social animals that respond to each other's sounds and develop complex hierarchies. The females lay hard-shelled eggs which are glued to walls or in crevices.

Skink-scaled Desert Gecko

Teratoscincus scincus

The Skink Gecko, which attains a length of 6 to 7 inches, is a member of one of the groups of ground geckos found in desert areas of central Asia. It digs shallow tunnel systems or hides under rocks, and the females lay their eggs in crevices. Most geckos have eyelids that are fused and transparent as do the snakes. Unlike snakes, they can protrude the large, flat tongue and wipe it over the outside of the eye, cleaning its surface.

Ground geckos walk with the body high off the ground. Those of desert regions often have wide feet like snowshoes that float and stabilize them on the surface of the sand. The wide scales on the tail of the Skink Gecko have very tiny projections that rub against each other, producing a faint hissing sound when the tail is rapidly bent from side to side. Since these geckos can also squeak and make sounds by blowing air through the mouth, we do not know the function of the hissing tail. Does it attract the insects on which the gecko feeds?

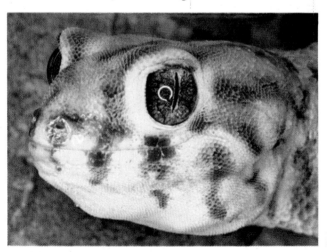

Black-headed Scaly Foot

Pygopus nigriceps

The fauna of Australia shows many differences from that of the adjacent Indo-Malaysian region. Obviously the continent was isolated for millennia, and the few animals that reached it were able to specialize with little competition. One such group were the pygopods (stump feet) or scaly feet of which this lizard is the one example.

Closely related to the geckos, the pygopods have become elongate (some up to 2 feet in length) and gradually reduced their limbs. Some show short stumps while others are completely limbless; this black-headed form has lost the front limbs, but retained well developed hindlimbs. The general tendency toward loss of limbs occurred separately in a number of other groups of lizards as well. Apparently elongation made it easier for some such animals to pass through narrow crevices, such as those in grass tussocks, by crawling. Crawling also costs much less energy than walking on limbs.

The slowly moving Black-headed Scaly Foot is a predator of arthropods. It is the largest pygopod found in the interior deserts of **56** Australia.

Granite Night Lizard
Xantusia henshawi

The night lizards are a small group resembling geckos in having fused eyelids and a vertical pupil that opens wide so they can see by starlight, but which closes to a slit during the day. These small lizards, which are less than 3 inches long, occupy a restricted area of Central America, the southwestern United States, and Cuba. Granite Night Lizards are one of four North American species restricted to southern California and Baja California.

They live on rocky outcrops and their blotched color pattern camouflages them well in their habitat. The Granite Night Lizard feeds on insects and gives birth to from one to three living young.

Common Iguana

Iguana iguana

The river forests of the tropical Americas are the home of these large green lizards. These animals grow to 6½ feet in length of which only a foot and a half is the body, the rest being the slender tail. The adults feed on plant material, while the juveniles hunt and eat insects.

Adult specimens often bask in high trees along river courses and will jump 18 to 20 feet into the water. They are excellent swimmers. The heavy dewlaps, irregular scales, and crest of spines along the back long made this one of Hollywood's favorite species for depicting prehistoric dragons.

Both the eggs and the flesh of the adult iguana are much prized as food, and in some districts of Central America it may be the most important game animal.

Marine Iguana

Amblyrhynchus cristatus

A number of large iguanas occur in various parts of the Americas. Perhaps the most curious of these large species is the Marine Iguana, which reaches a total length of 5 feet and, at one time, occurred in enormous numbers on the rocky shores of the volcanic Galápagos Islands. Several local races occurred, varying in—among other things —the amount of brick-red blotching the sides of the body.

The Marine Iguana is primarily vegetarian, feeding on marine algae both when these are exposed at low tide and by grazing underwater. The animals swim very well, folding the arms against the body, which moves by slow undulation. The salt taken in as part of their diet is discharged from the blood by special glands on the side of the face.

The Galápagos Islands are also inhabited by a large Land Iguana and by several small, terrestrial species.

▲ Common Iguana ▼ Marine Iguana (Galápagos)

Chuckwalla

Sauromalus obesus

This lizard of rocky deserts is spectacularly adapted for survival in the dry environments of the southwestern United States. Not only does the Chuckwalla have a highly impervious skin that loses little water in respiration, but it also has water sacs beneath the skin that provide storage from times when water-rich vegetation is available. Chuckwallas comfortably survive temperatures of 45°C (113°F), which would be fatal for most mammals, including man. When threatened, this lizard wedges itself into rock crevices and then inflates the body with air so that it cannot be pulled out until it relaxes.

Chuckwallas feed mainly on plant materials, though juveniles take small insects as well. A large specimen of this lizard can reach 18 inches.

Anole eating Cricket

Common Anole

Anolis carolinensis

The anoles are small to medium-sized (7 inches maximum), mainly arboreal lizards that have become immensely successful. More than 300 species range from the southeastern United States through the humid tropics into Brazil. Once this anole was the only United States species, but some half-dozen other Latin American forms have recently been introduced into southern Florida.

Where several species occur in the same place, one is apt to occupy the ground and low grasses, while another may occupy the trunks or canopy of palms and trees. Even males and females occupy different locations. The males display to each other by bobbing the body up and down and showing a brightly colored scarlet or yellow throat fan. Anoles used to be sold as pets under the name of "American chameleons."

Intensive study of these common and easily observed animals is teaching herpetologists a great deal about the way in which reptiles invade new areas and how new species arise.

Forest Iguana

Polychrus gutturosus

The anoles or false chameleons of the Americas show numerous relatives in the various South American forest regions. This Costa Rican species lives in the forest regions of Central America. The tail tends to be three times as long as the 4- to 6-inch body and serves as a balancing organ when the animal climbs, rather slowly, in the forest canopy. The extensive toes of the widely spread hindlimbs let the lizard clasp branches. Thus these animals can retain a firm grip with the hindlimbs when only these are in contact with a branch.

Several species of the group show some sexual dimorphism in coloration. In such forms the males are characterized by almost uniform dark green to brownish patterns, while the females are marked in various patterns of browns, whites, and blacks having the capacity to become green when excited.

Numerous other genera of forest iguanas occur in South America with each type represented by only a few species in a generally restricted range. These small lizards feed on arboreal insects and all lay eggs in the ground.

Eastern Fence Lizard

Sceloporus undulatus

The various fence lizards are also known as spiny lizards, so called as each scale of their body bears a keel that terminates in a sharp, backward-projecting point. This is the common iguanid of the eastern and central United States, where it is found on rock and wooden fences and the boles of trees.

Fence lizards grow to 3 inches in head and body length with the tail about half as long again. They climb well on rough surfaces onto which their claws can catch hold.

As in many other iguanid lizards the males have a distinctive coloration, in this case brilliant-blue regions on the throat and the sides of the belly. It is interesting to note that while these signal colors can be displayed to passing fence lizards, they are in relatively well-hidden places on the body and are unlikely to be perceived by a predator looking down from above.

Coast Horned Lizard

Phrynosoma coronatum

The 3- to 7-inch-long horned lizards are the American (iguanid) equivalent of the Australian Moloch (an agamid) and reflect the convergent
evolution of similar body shapes and life histories in different lines living
on different continents. Fifteen species range over most of the southwestern United States and far south into Mexico.

These are diurnal species that feed on insects, some of them having
specialized on ants which are avoided by most other kinds of lizards.
Several species of horned lizards can survive for long periods, even in
deserts, without free water by making use of the nightly dew.

Some species can rupture a blood vessel in their eye and spray the
resulting fluid for some inches. Apparently this greatly disconcerts such
64 predators as coyotes, which tend to avoid them.

Mountain Iguana
Liolaemus ornatus

Some 70 species of these small iguanids occupy the Andes Mountains and more inland regions south from the equator to Tierra del Fuego. Various forms live in desert valleys or open plains; others ascend the ridges rising from 9,000 to 15,000 feet. The 6-inch Mountain Iguana lives far above the tree and even the vegetation line in the screes just beneath ridges across which the wind blows continuously.

Apparently, these iguanids feed on aerial plankton, small airborne arthropods, dropped off here by the air currents and in turn feeding on the mosses and lichens that are the only plants in this inhospitable environment.

These small, live-bearing lizards manage to keep their body temperature some 30° above that of their surroundings by directly capturing the sun's energy by basking. Some lowland species continue to lay eggs.

Plumed Basilisk

Basiliscus plumifrons

The basilisk was a mythical crowned animal, and these small lizards inherited the name because of their casque-like heads. They are medium-sized—up to 30-inch-long—iguanas of the river rain forests of central and northern South America, and naturalists' interest rests on more than mythology.

Their main specialization derives from running across the surface of the water without sinking. The Basilisk's toes are long and each is provided with a flap along the outside; the flap opens when the foot hits the water. While this imposes a certain resistance during the down-stroke, the flap immediately closes when the foot reverses so that the toe can be withdrawn with little resistance. Small animals have been observed to run for hundreds of feet across the water surfaces; larger lizards run for shorter distances, obviously with more effort. Basilisks can also swim and do so with facility. The water walking allows them a rapid escape from enemies on land without the risk of being eaten by fishes or caimans that might lurk in the waters.

Common Agama
Agama agama

Agamids are the Old World equivalents of the iguanids of the New World. The Common Agama ranges far across the African continent. The genus has 60 species, some of which range through Asia; a few species grow to be 18 inches long, but the average size is about 12 inches. The Common Agamas are the ubiquitous diurnal lizards of Africa, and one sees them on tree trunks, rock faces, fences, and the walls of houses.

The head is yellow or orange, particularly in adult males. The body is brownish to bluish black, the color varying between local populations.

Agamas are highly territorial. The males interact regularly, displaying to each other from elevated perches bobbing up and down and, in some cases, inflating or erecting the throat fan.

Most species feed on insects, though the larger individuals of some forms take flowers and leaves.

67

Princely Mastigure
Uromastyx princeps

The mastigures are a group of large lizards, several species of which exceed 2 feet in length, that range from West Central Africa to India. All are characterized by a blunt head and a long tail covered with rings of thorn-like scales. The prettiest is the small Princely Mastigure of Somalia, which is only 6 inches long and beautifully colored in green, orange, and black.

All mastigures are desert dwellers and feed primarily on buds, leaves, and twigs, which they trim off with the sharp teeth edging their jaws. They can produce moisture from plant material and consequently **68** survive for months and even years without drinking.

Moloch

Moloch horridus

This curious lizard, about 6 inches long, occupies some of the driest regions in the center of Australia. Its grotesque appearance leads to a name which does injustice to this harmless creature. The lizard's shape and color provide a camouflage matching the background. Apparently the animal feeds only on live ants and is, consequently, most difficult to keep in captivity.

Its adaptation to a desert environment is extreme: not only can it avoid drinking for long periods but it also has a microscopic striation of the skin covering the head scales, allowing it to utilize dew which, by capillary action, flows down these minute ridges to the edges of the mouth and is then swallowed. The Moloch thus occupies the same place among the agamids as the horned lizard does among the iguanids.

Blood Sucker

Calotes versicolor

The tree agamas, to which the inappropriately named and harmless Blood Sucker belongs, range from Afghanistan to New Guinea well across the Indo-Malaysian region.

The males of this highly arboreal group of lizards are a rust brown except when they are excited during the mating season, when the head of the 16-inch-long Blood Sucker assumes a brilliant-scarlet color as the males display to each other. The sight of two males rushing around palm trunks while bobbing at each other and flashing their throat flaps is truly impressive.

Most tree agamas feed on insects and lay eggs which are buried in the ground. All of them are diurnal.

Australian Bearded Lizard

Amphibolurus barbatus

Many agamas resemble iguanas in having erectable dewlaps which course down the middle of the throat. The bearded lizard has gone this one better and spreads the cartilages of the throat into a horizontal fan that may be stretched in all directions. While iguanas generally place themselves sideways to one another during display, the bearded lizards display head-on. They open their mouth wide, gasp, and jump forward with throat fan extended.

They are relatively large lizards, about 2½ feet long. Several related species occur over all of Australia except in the extreme north. The females produce between eight and 27 eggs which are buried in a hole much deeper than the animal is long. Young bearded lizards feed on insects; as they mature, they take first lizards and rodents and then plant material.

Like some other lizards, these agamids can warm up much faster than they cool down, as they selectively pump their blood through the warm portions of the skin and slow down the blood-flow through cool areas.

▼ Rib cage expanded for gliding

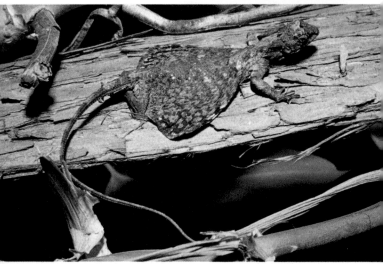

Asiatic Flying Lizard

Draco sp.

The forests of the Indo-Malaysian region are inhabited by some half-dozen species of agamid lizards that glide effectively. These small (snout-to-tail length 6 inches), arboreal animals have their ribs elongated and are provided with muscles that can spread them, stretching a loose membrane and making their body almost circular in plan when viewed from the top. With limbs and tail extended, these animals can plane from one tree trunk to another. Upon approaching a tree, they twist the body into a stall that kills forward motion and lands them head up. In some cases, bright color patches are visible during flight, while the resting coloration is dull and provides excellent camouflage.

Common Chameleon

Chameleo vulgaris

This south Mediterranean species is a typical representative of a group of lizards that ranges into south central Asia and across Africa to the Cape of Good Hope. Derived from agamids, chameleons have become specialized for living in trees. Both hands and feet have opposed fingers and toes, letting them grasp narrow twigs. The body, from 8 to 10 inches long, is flattened and the tail prehensile, promoting stability when the wind ruffles bushes and trees. Color-change mechanisms in the skin of some species match the surface appearance to that of the surroundings by changing from brownish to greenish hues.

Most remarkable is the feeding method. The tongue can be projected as far as a full body's length and then pulled back, carrying insects trapped on its sticky tip.

Demonstration of the Chameleon's rotating eyes

Three-horned Chameleon

Chameleo jacksoni

Certain East African chameleons have horns on their snout reminding one of the much larger fossil reptiles known as ceratopsians. Some species have horns in both sexes; in others, horns are restricted to males. It was once argued that such horns, flaps, and ridges lacked a function, but we now know that they serve as species-recognition signals during courtship displays. Only 4 inches long, the males of this East African chameleon use their horns in fighting: they meet on a narrow branch and lock horns until the stronger dislodges his opponent.

Short-tailed Dwarf Chameleon
Rhampholeon marshalli

Most of the true chameleons tend to have a greenish color, at least part of the time. In contrast, the dwarf chameleons, 3 to 4 inches long, are mainly brownish, though some of them show markings on the sides of the body, which give them the appearance of dead leaves. This coloration makes it clear that these chameleons have descended to the ground and, secondarily, become terrestrial. They have retained the curious grasping foot but lack the prehensile tail.

Native to Central Africa, including Madagascar, dwarf chameleons can sometimes be found under rocks. Some prefer cooler temperatures than the tree chameleons: instead of values near 30°C (86°F) one observes levels near 28°C (82°F). While they prefer ground localities, these animals can climb and do ascend small bushes when hunting their insect prey.

Blue-tongued Skink

Tiliqua scincoides

The skinks are a group of semi-burrowing lizards that mostly have a smooth skin with the soft part of each scale formed over an internal bony plate. They have a vast distribution reaching all continents, particularly in the tropical areas. The group is so enormous that it has been recently suggested that there are actually four subgroups of skinks that are only superficially related. The Blue-tongued Skink of Australia reaches lengths up to 20 inches. While it is quite sizable, it is small compared to the giant skink of Madagascar, which became extinct about 300 years ago.

It is a good hunter of snails and insects and also eats fruits. It is much more active than would appear from its sausage-like surface shape. Like most skinks, it is a diurnal animal.

Females give birth to six to 20 live young.

African Snake Skink
Riopa sundevalli

The tendency of many of the skinks to live below the soil's surface has led to independent reduction of limbs in several groups. It is not clear whether some of the animals so specialized really spend most of their life underground, resulting in a reduced reliance on limbs for locomotion or stabilization.

The body of this 6- to 10-inch-long snake skink has become long enough to make lateral undulation an effective motor mechanism. The elongation has, however, proceeded quite differently from that seen in amphisbaenians: rather than stretching out the body, skinks have tended to extend the tail, and, in many species, the diameter of the tail is almost identical to that of the body. The curves of the trunk may then pass smoothly onto the tail and the tail may also assist propulsion, increasing the effective length of these animals. In many skinks the tail also houses large strips of fat providing energy storage that may be used during the reproductive period. **77**

Jeweled Lacerta

Lacerta lepida

Lacertas are ground lizards of various sizes that are often excellent runners and climbers over rocks and sand. Their color varies from blacks and brown into greens and sometimes, as in the jeweled species of the Mediterranean area, with blue portholes. These lizards have a complex mating behavior which has been studied extensively, and related species lay eggs or bear live young.

One member of this group ranges north of the Arctic Circle. Many of the small islands of the Mediterranean and Adriatic are inhabited by characteristic forms, and this situation has provided another natural laboratory of speciation similar to that represented by the anoles in the Americas.

Lacertas are diurnal and remarkably adapted to varied conditions in relatively small areas. At almost 30 inches, the Jeweled Lacerta is one of the largest among the Lacertidae.

Banded Tegu
Tupinambis teguixin

The teiids are the American equivalent of the European-Asian-African lacertas. Some members of the two groups are so similar superficially that it takes a specialist to tell the difference between them. Other members of the teiids, such as the very large species, do not have equivalents among the lacertids.

The Banded Tegu is perhaps the largest teiid. It occupies a very extensive range from the Guianas across the lowlands of tropical South America to Argentina. Like most other large lizards, it supplements its diet of mammals, birds, and lizards with insects and worms as well as fruits and leaves. This lizard is much stouter and heavier than, for instance, the iguana; the 4½-foot specimen collected by one biologist weighed about ten pounds.

All this suggests that tegus are ground-living rather than arboreal. They can climb and do lay their eggs in the arboreal nests of tree termites. Not only do these termites quickly repair the opening into which the eggs have been laid, but the soldier termites presumably defend the nest against predators.

Caiman Lizard

Dracaena guianensis

·The 4-foot Caiman Lizard is primarily aquatic, as are a few of the smaller teiids. It occupies rivers, small streams, and swamps, and swims quite well. This is a diurnal lizard which rests on land at night and spends the day in the water.

While some of the other water teiids feed on small fishes, tadpoles, and frogs, the Caiman Lizard subsists exclusively on aquatic snails, some so large that they can just be grasped with the mouth wide open. Such snails are carefully maneuvered to the back of the mouth and crushed between the posterior teeth of each row. Unlike the front teeth—indeed all of the teeth of other teiids—the back teeth of Caiman Lizards have enormous rounded crowns, and the shells are crushed between these. The animal then carefully separates shell from soft parts with its tongue and wipes shell fragments out of the mouth before swallowing the snail.

Yellow-throated Plated Lizard

Gerrhosaurus flavigularis

The gerrhosaurids are terrestrial lizards that range widely across Africa, occupying mainly savanna and open areas and not entering the forests. The group is represented on Madagascar.

The Yellow-throated Plated Lizard is a bit over 18 inches long, lays eggs, and feeds mostly on arthropods. It is remarkably shy for such a large animal.

The scales of its body are quite regularly arranged and each has a heavy bony core similar to that found in skinks. The armor is heavy and the scales interlock, providing a solid protection that probably deters the attacks of smaller enemies. This family again shows the common trend toward elongation, and some of the South African species have lost the front limbs.

Sungazer or Giant Zonure

Cordylus giganteus

This club-tailed lizard of southern Africa is the largest member of its group, reaching about 15 inches in size. Its head is spined, the back plated, and the tail covered with rings of half-inch-long bone-cored spines. Only the belly scales are unprotected; when threatened, these animals will stretch out on the ground holding the limbs against the sides and vigorously resisting any effort to turn them onto their back.

The closely related Armadillo Lizard does the Sungazer one better by rolling up into a ball when disturbed: whichever way one rotates the ball one encounters only the spiny armor.

All of these lizards are live-bearers, giving birth to two 5-inch-long young at a time. Sungazers are carnivores.

Imperial Flat Lizard
Platysaurus imperator

The savanna areas of southern Africa are interspersed with bare granite outcrops that sometimes rise to heights of hundreds of feet. Weathered-rock slides accumulate around their edges and these as well as the crevices of the rock face are the home of the flat lizards. They remind one of the Chuckwallas among the iguanids in their ability to lock themselves into crevices by inflating the body.

Unlike the Armored Zonures, the male flat lizards are often brightly colored with carmine set off with black, green, and blue areas.

These foot-long, egg-laying flat lizards feed primarily on grasshoppers and beetles, which they hunt during the day. Their social behavior is only now being studied.

Snake-like Girdle Tail

Chamaesaura aenea

The girdle-tailed lizards would seem to be the least likely species to have limbless relatives; this makes the present assemblage of South African snake lizards so interesting. Perhaps four species of the elongate (16- to 25-inch) Snake-like Girdle Tails have been described. These show a gradual progression from five digits to two, to one, while the last species lacks any external front limbs. The scales of the body are heavily keeled and the keels align into ridges.

Clearly these animals are not burrowers. Instead they resemble some of the Australian pygopods in inhabiting grass tussocks where they hunt small insects and other animal prey.

Like the zonures, but unlike the flat lizards, these elongate cordylids hold their eggs until ready to hatch.

Shedding skin

Giant Glass Lizard or Scheltopusik
Ophisaurus apodus

The anguid lizards range across all continents except Australia and show their greatest diversity in the Americas. Many of the species are limbless as this Scheltopusik (a Slavic word meaning "yellow belly"). This is an enormous lizard with large specimens reaching almost 5 feet in length and more than 2 inches in diameter. Only wart-like remnants of the hind limbs are evident and no forelimbs remain.

These large lizards seem to feed preferably on land snails which they crush and eat, shell remnants and all. Lacking limbs, they clean the face by wiping the sides of the head against the ground. Recent feeding studies in agricultural areas of southern Russia suggest that these lizards are a very important factor in the biological control of insect pests. Apparently they preferably feed on corn beetles.

The Scheltopusik ranges from the Balkans to central Asia. Specimens have lived for 20 years in a terrarium, but the related European Slow-worm is supposed to have lived more than 35 years in captivity. **85**

California Legless Lizard

Anniella pulchra

The coastal regions of southern California and Baja California are the home of these legless lizards, a term that by now will be seen to have minimal descriptive value.

These lizards, which are 8 to 10 inches long, occupy loose sandy areas and have become sand swimmers rather than burrowers. They pass through the sands by lateral undulation, detecting their prey mainly by smell both underground and at the surface. Like the amphisbaenians, these snake lizards require a fairly humid soil and will often dig down to levels at which the soil starts to be moist.

Like many other limbless lizards these are live-bearing; the young become sexually mature in three years.

Gila Monster and Mexican Beaded Lizard

Heloderma suspectum and *H. horridum*

Although these two lizards are quite closely related, they are both shown because they represent the *only* poisonous lizards in the world. Certain varanids do show some enzymes in their saliva but none is even mildly poisonous. The Gila Monster is found in the extreme southwestern United States starting from southern Nevada and southeastern Utah to Sonora; the Mexican species ranges south, almost to the Guatemalan border.

These medium-sized animals—total length being about 2 feet for the northern and almost 3 feet for the southern form—are quite stout and easily recognized by the blunt head, fat, rounded tail, and scales that appear as if the surface were raised into pebbles. Both spend much of the day in tunnels or crevices and emerge at dusk to hunt for the young of ground-nesting birds, small mammals, and reptiles.

The teeth of both the upper and lower jaws are fluted and show deep grooves on their outside. The glands of the lower lip produce a potent venom which has to be introduced into prey by chewing action. While the venom is very effective for small mammals there appear to have been no human fatalities directly attributable to bites. However, even though most human victims recover, it is clear that these animals should be treated with great caution.

▲ California Legless Lizard

▲Gila Monster ▼ Mexican Beaded Lizard

Komodo Dragon

Varanus komodoensis

The Komodo Dragons are monitors that are now restricted to a few islands in Indonesia. It is hoped that they will be protected there because they are not only the largest surviving lizards, but a truly spectacular group. Their habits have recently been studied and prove to be different from those of the smaller species of the large group of monitor lizards. From the 1½ inch-long eggs these animals grow to a length well over 10 feet, and such large specimens are capable of immobilizing, killing, and dismembering small deer and wild pigs. A 9-foot specimen has been observed to grab a 4-footer and break its back by a single shake of the head.

Like all monitors the Komodo Dragon has a curved row of very sharp, backward-curving teeth. Small prey is grabbed and shaken so violently that the body cavity may rupture and pieces be separated off. Larger prey is broken by being bitten while the forelimbs tear and scratch the protruding parts.

Nile Monitor

Varanus niloticus

The Nile Monitor ranges from Senegal to Somalia and from Egypt to South Africa. Only the true desert and some large forests are inhabited by other species. It is a large form exceeding 6 feet in length and extremely common in some savanna localities and along river courses. Like many other monitors it is an excellent swimmer, moving by lateral undulation with the limbs pressed against the sides of the body.

These monitors feed on a variety of small mammals, snakes, and lizards, but their most spectacular prey is the Nile Crocodile. They are well-known nest-robbers, searching out the river banks and digging out crocodile egg pockets as well as preying on the hatchlings.

Sand Goanna

Varanus gouldi

The name goanna is a corruption of the Carib word iguana, here applied to a monitor lizard. While the largest of the monitors occur in Africa and Asia, and the Nile Monitor clearly has the largest geographical distribution, there are almost as many species in Australia as in the rest of the world combined.

The loose articulation between the tip of the monitor's lower jaws, as well as the solidly joined brain case and some other specializations, suggest to herpetologists that monitors may well be close to the sorts of animals that must have given rise to snakes. This becomes plausible when looking at such slender-headed Australian species as the Sand Goanna. While these species are clearly very long, they are relatively more slender than some of the Asiatic forms. What seems much more important is that they have a considerably longer and snake-like neck, which they pull into an S-shaped curve when they dart at prey.

Bornean Earless Monitor
Lanthanotus borneensis

This small, dark-brown earless lizard was, in 1960, known from a half-dozen specimens taken during three-quarters of a century. Just one year later, an anthropological field party discovered another specimen in Sarawak, Northern Borneo. Literally dozens of specimens have since turned up in the same area, and we now have a far better understanding of their life history and anatomy. The results confirm that they lie close to the group from which snakes arose.

These monitors clearly are half-subterranean: they live in the soil adjacent to forests where they make tunnels that end beneath decaying vegetation. Earless monitors swim freely and are apparently caught regularly in fishtraps and in the canals around rice paddies. They feed on worms and probably on fishes, to judge from a zookeeper's report that his specimens liked to feed on "filet of sole." **91**

Snakes

Western Slender Blind Snake
Leptotyphlops humilis

The Slender Blind Snake belongs to one of three families of small, cylindrical, glossy snakes that spend most of their life underground, generally in association with colonies of ants and termites.

They retain vestiges of the pelvic girdle but all traces of external limbs have disappeared. The head has been structured for burrowing by having the anterior edge rounded and the mouth shifted to the lower surface. The jaws are very small and the teeth are found only on the lower pair. In the true blind snakes the scales have very large free edges so that any one overlaps the bases of the next three in a row.

Their shiny surface provides good protection against the bites of some insects: the sharp jaws of the attacker just glance off the smooth armor. These snakes also produce secretions in their cloacal glands which deter the attacks of the ants with which they associate and on which they feed.

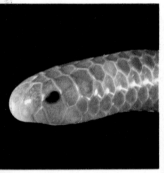

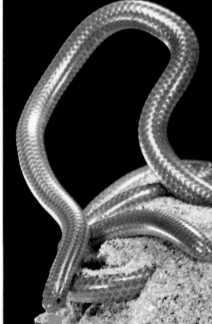

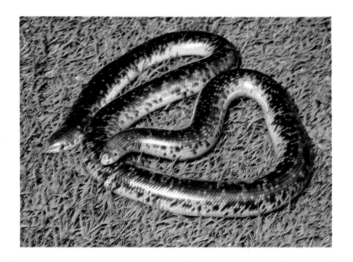

Giant Blind Snake

Typhlops schlegelli

Although these blind snakes (or Typhlopidae) live underground, they show only limited specializations for burrowing. They differ from the Slender Blind Snakes (or Leptotyphlopidae) by having teeth only on the upper jaws and also by a more irregular series of connecting muscles between skin and backbone.

The Giant Blind Snake of Africa, which grows to be almost 3 feet long, has the upper surface of the head rounded but the bottom flattened. The sharp, U-shaped edge so formed is used to pierce the wall between galleries of termite nests. The trunk is rounded, but the animal's middle is much stouter than the ends, suggesting that widening of underground tunnels does not cost them too much energy: perhaps they prefer softer soils or existing tunnel systems.

This species and its relatives range over much of Africa, while other blind snakes are found all around the world. Indeed one small blind snake has become so well established in agricultural areas of southeast Asia that it is regularly transported to oceanic islands and has now reached Hawaii, apparently from the Philippines. **93**

Red-blotched Shield Tail

Uropeltis rubromaculatus

The moist mountain forests of India and Sri Lanka (Ceylon) are occupied by the shield tails, which include some 43 kinds of beautifully marked, burrowing snakes that seem to subsist mainly on earthworms and the grubs of insects.

The dorsal surface of these foot-long snakes is generally dark, but the sides of the body show a series of bright-colored, orange-yellow blotches or triangles. The end of the tail often shows bright rings and spots. The head is pointed and the tail blunt, giving the false impression, at first glance, that the head is the tail and the tail the head. When disturbed on the surface, shield tails tend to coil about bits of grass, twigs, and even fingers. In doing so they hide the head and stretch out the tail, moving it about to attract attention. The tail tip bears a spiny shield that collects particles of mud to protect the snake when a predator tries to bite.

Blyth's Lankan Shield Tail
Rhinophis blythi

These shield-tailed snakes of the island of Sri Lanka (Ceylon) are burrowers with a sharply pointed nose bearing a keratinized ridge that allows them to penetrate more easily between stems and roots of moist soil. Each push extending their tunnel is followed by the formation of an S-curve in the neck, thus increasing the tunnel's diameter.

The mountain forests that were once their home have largely been destroyed, and most of the species of this group now survive in kitchen gardens amid the tea plantations and in other irrigated agricultural areas. Here these foot-long snakes feed on worms and insect larvae and give birth to live young. Like some other reptiles, the shield tails have become commensal, or dependent on man.

South American Pipe Snake

Anilius scytale

The forests of northern South America are the home of this beautifully colored ground snake. Related to the pipe snakes of Asia, and through them to the shield tails and to the boids, the South American Pipe Snake has a number of primitive characteristics. Among these are the very solid vertebrae and the heavy skull that let them tunnel through the soil and overcome small rodents and snakes by biting and constriction.

These beautifully red-and-black-banded animals, which reach a length of about 30 inches, are fond of the water and some of their specializations may be aquatic rather than burrowing. When disturbed the snake spreads its ribs to the sides and flattens its body. Simultaneously, it waves its tail upward in a curve which displays the even brighter red and black ventral surface as a warning signal.

Blotched Pipe Snake

Cylindrophis maculatus

Closely related to the South American Pipe Snake is a group of some three species of snakes that occur in eastern Asia from Sri Lanka (Ceylon) to Indonesia. These are definitely burrowing animals that feed on rodents and ground reptiles, which they catch within tunnel systems. Recent studies demonstrate that their heavy and rigid jaws allow them to crush the prey as well as kill it by constriction. Consequently they show a functional analog to the feeding patterns of amphisbaenians.

The Blotched Pipe Snake of Sri Lanka is the smallest—usually less than 20 inches long—most elegantly marked member of the group and occurs in all formerly forested parts of the island. This species may feed on limbless amphibians as does its South American relative.

▼ *Cylindrophis rufus* ▲ *Cylindrophis maculatus*

Sunbeam Snake

Xenopeltis unicolor

The Sunbeam Snake, a large snake of the Indo-Malaysian region, is a chocolate-brown to black snake that reaches 3 feet in length. Its skull is quite stout, but its lower jaw is significantly more flexible than that of the pipe snakes. Unlike many of the advanced snakes which have only one lung, the Sunbeam Snake still has two, but it lacks the pelvic girdle.

Its scales are highly polished and overlapping, thus providing minimum friction with the soil and little space for lodgment of dirt or parasites on the outside surface. The polish derives from the way the surface cells of the skin lay down the keratin. As in some other burrowing snakes, this involves microscopic parallel ridges oriented along the snake's length. The ridges act as a diffraction grating so that this normally unicolored brown snake shines in the colors of the rainbow when sunlight strikes it, hence its popular name.

Elephant Trunk Snake

Acrochordus javanicus

Two species of wart snakes inhabit the coasts of eastern Asia and the Indo-Malaysian region. Of these the Elephant Trunk Snake is found in the eastern half of the range. These are most curious-looking animals, as their skin appears to be draped in loose folds, particularly when the snake is exposed on mud flats after the tide has receded. The skin used to be made into specialty leather known as *karung*.

In the water, Elephant Trunk Snakes are far more graceful: they swim effectively and seem to move along without effort. To do so they flatten the body, pulling the sides together into a vertical band. Unlike those of most snakes, their scales are conical and apparently used to hold onto slippery fishes which they catch between coils of their body. In all other snakes the intestine runs more or less straight down the length of the body, but the Elephant Trunk Snake has a coiled small intestine. If unwound the intestine of a 3-foot snake would measure more than 6 feet. **99**

Boa Constrictor

Boa constrictor

The boid snakes include boas and pythons, the former found mostly in the New World and the latter in the Old. The Boa Constrictor is the boid snake most commonly seen in captivity and perhaps best known. Tens of thousands of young specimens collected in South America have been imported into the United States as pets. Fewer than one out of a thousand ultimately grows large enough to become a problem to the owner and is then donated to the local zoo. Most boas reared in captivity remain stunted and do not reach the 18- to 19-foot maximum length of wild adults.

The Boa Constrictor feeds mostly on birds, its long teeth permitting it to penetrate the thick coat of feathers. As the name implies, this beautiful snake of the tropical American forests kills its prey by constriction. Like other constrictors it responds to the minor vibrations produced by the pulsing heart and keeps the coils around its prey until the beat stops. The pressure applied does not break any bones and the food object is swallowed in its entirety.

The Boa Constrictor gives birth to live young.

▲ Common Boa Constrictor
Red-tailed Boa ▶

Emerald Tree Boa

Corallus caninus

The South American Emerald Tree Boa is one of the most beautiful of the boas. Its rich green dorsal color is relieved by white bands or cross marks, and the yellow ventral color extends onto the upper lip. This 4-foot-long snake is a true tree boa and will rest coiled in a series of half-loops that droop down on both sides of a branch.

All of its feeding occurs in trees, where it captures lizards and birds using the temperature-sensitive pits that lie between the scales of the upper and lower lip to help aim the strike.

The young, which are born alive, are a reddish brown and look quite unlike the adults: they do not become green until they are a little over 2 feet in length.

▼ Rosy Boa ▲ Rubber Boa

Rubber Boa

Charina bottae

The western United States is the home of two small crepuscular (hiding) boas that range up to about 2 feet in length. These shy animals live on or below ground, burrowing in loose soil. Both give birth to living young and differ mainly in their color patterns. The Rosy Boa has a striped body, while the Rubber Boa is of a uniform greenish-brown color without a pattern, giving it a rubbery appearance. The Rubber Boa is found along the Pacific Coast from Mexico to Washington and eastward into Montana.

When disturbed, these small, inoffensive rodent-eaters will roll up into a ball, hiding the head in the center. Both are excellent climbers, using concertina movement with part of the body fixed while the rest is being pushed along.

Green Tree Python

Chondropython viridis

This tree python, about 5 feet in length, is found only in New Guinea, and only a herpetologist can tell it apart from the Emerald Tree Boa with which it has no connection. One differentiating characteristic is that the temperature-sensitive pits in this python are positioned in the center of each lip scale rather than between scales.

Both species are obviously adapted for life in trees, and consequently one sees extreme parallelism in the coloration, in the way the animals drape themselves over branches when resting, and even in the appearance and reddish color of the juveniles. Since the ancestral forms in each case were quite different, this phenomenon is called "convergence" by biologists.

▲ Asiatic Ground Boa ▼ Anaconda

Asiatic Ground Boa

Eryx conicus

The deserts and plains of western Asia are the home of the burrowing ground boas that preferentially feed on rodents and lizards and spend most of their life underground. These snakes, which are 2 to 4 feet long, may be identified by their very short, conical tail and perfectly cylindrical body.

Their habitat ranges from desert regions of Iran to the moist plains of southern India, with the desert species capable of surviving for months without drinking. In the agricultural areas of southern India these snakes are extremely common. Here they occupy tunnels in the dikes between the rice paddies as well as in the stone piles alongside fields, and are probably a major factor in the control of rodents that feed on the crops.

Anaconda

Eunectes murinus

The great rivers of South America are the home of this boa, the largest of all snakes. Not only does it probably hold the record for length—with a total of about 37 to 38 feet—but clearly the record for weight, since an adult northern Anaconda 30 feet long would be over 2 feet in diameter, and such an animal would weigh at least half a ton. Since river and swampy regions often make it difficult or impossible to perceive the entire length of an animal, there are numerous tales of Anacondas much larger than those for which proper records have been taken.

The Anaconda is essentially a water snake though specimens have been observed basking in trees or on the shores of river courses. It feeds on fishes, aquatic mammals, water birds, and the South American caiman, always constricting the prey first.

Carpet Python
Morelia spilotes

Several races of these beautiful pythons, which grow to 6 to 8 feet in length, range over most of Australia. In photographs, their beautiful red and yellow blotched pattern, variegated with black, seems to stand out sharply, but actually it blends into the background when the animal is resting among shrubbery.

   Carpet Pythons are important factors in the control of birds and small mammals, such as rabbits, which they hunt mostly at night, searching both in underground warrens and in trees. Like most other pythons, they are egg-layers.

Ball Python

Python regius

This beautiful small ground python is restricted to the forest and savanna regions of coastal West Africa. It feeds almost exclusively on rodents and is considered sacred and hence protected by the people of Dahomey: one of the first treaties between the British and the kings of Nigeria contained a clause specifically assuring the security of various pythons.

When disturbed, the snake throws its firm muscular body into a ball-like coil with the head resting on the inside, accounting for its popular name. Ball Pythons lay eggs.

Reticulated Python
Python reticulatus

Africa, India, and the Indo-Malaysian archipelago are inhabited by giant pythons. The Reticulated Python of the latter region is by far the longest; it reaches documented lengths of at least 33 feet.

Like most pythons, the Reticulated Python lays eggs, and the size of the clutch increases with the length of the mother, the largest recorded clutch size being near 100.

All pythons kill their prey by constriction, and there are a few records of attacks on man, mostly involving children or women. Although there are records of large specimens eating 100-pound pigs, it is unlikely that even a 25-foot snake could swallow an adult man, though it might be able to kill one.

African Rock Python

Python sebae

This beautiful animal, with neatly defined brown, black, and yellow patterns on the back, occupies a wide range in the African savanna and forest country. It attains a length of 16-18 feet and has been reported to feed on anything from lizards to birds and even small antelopes, although most wild specimens subsist on small rodents.

Like most other boid snakes, the rock python has a series of heat-sensitive pits on the sides of the face that are able to sense passing warm-blooded prey. The pits of both sides are used to triangulate and aim a strike accurately, even in complete darkness.

The Indian and African pythons have been observed to brood their eggs, coiling around them and by continuous twitching of their muscles raising their temperature by a few degrees, thus incubating them until they hatch.

Cuban Ground Boa

Tropidophis melanurus

Eleven species of ground boas range through the large islands of the Antilles and into South America, various related species occurring on the mainland of South America. All are beautifully marked in varying shades of brown and yellow and have a stout body, gradually tapering to a thin neck and tail. The head is elongate and noticeably triangular. The Cuban species is barely 3 feet long. These snakes are harmless to man and feed mainly on small reptiles and mammals, which they kill by constriction.

Some species of ground boa defend themselves by a mechanism which has been described but is not yet understood: when disturbed, the snake can apparently rupture a blood vessel near its tear gland; the blood flushes down the tear duct, passing underneath the fused transparent eyelids, and then out of the mouth. Human observers note that the eye turns bright red, and the blood then drips from the mouth. Nothing is known either about the chemistry of this apparently defensive secretion or about the predator toward whom it is directed.

Bull Snake

Pituophis melanoleucus

The Bull Snakes range throughout most of the United States. These large animals often exceed 7 feet in length and feed almost entirely on small mammals of which they may be one of the more important controlling factors. The Bull Snakes climb and burrow and have been observed to dig rodents out of their tunnels by shifting the soil from the hole with loops of their body.

Their name derives from their pugnacious habit: when attacked or disturbed they do not immediately retreat but strike at the intruder by vibrating their tail, simultaneously exhaling sharply. The air stream inflates and vibrates a little fold of soft tissue in the front of the mouth, producing a loud hiss. (Contrary to the widely-held belief, relatively few snakes hiss.)

111

Rat Snake

Elaphe obsoleta

Many pictured sequences have shown cases of convergence, the phenomenon in which different animals that live in similar environments, such as branches of forest trees or holes in the ground, show similar characteristics. This species of Rat Snake shows the opposite tendency, as specimens taken in different parts of the United States show almost no resemblance to each other. This Rat Snake, which ranges in size from 4 to 9 feet, extends widely over North America from New England south to the tip of Florida and Texas and west to Minnesota, Nebraska, Kansas, Oklahoma, and Texas.

The "black rat snake" of the northeastern states gradually changes into the "grey rat snake" and "Texas rat snake" in which the back is brownish and saddles of a darker color follow each other along the dorsal surface. Most striking is the change that occurs near the northern part of Florida where the Rat Snake becomes yellow, has four dark stripes marching down the back to the tail, and is locally called the "four-lined chicken snake."

Until careful study showed that the population changed gradually, the black rat and the four-lined chicken snakes were considered to belong to different species. The juveniles of all of these forms resemble one another much more than do the adults: when the eggs hatch, all hatchlings have a series of dorsal blotches, and only later do they assume the adult coloration of either a yellow background with black bands or a shiny black—the result of further pigment deposition. Adult Rat Snakes feed on birds and rodents and are excellent climbers, often stemming their way by concertina motion along the rough bark of trees.

Black rat snake

Black rat snake: ▲ hatching ▲ young

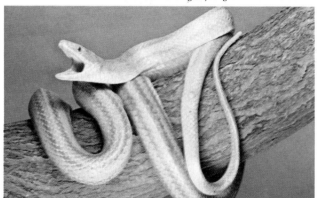

▲ Four-lined chicken snake ▼ Grey rat snake

Dhaman

Ptyas mucosus

These rat snakes, attaining lengths of nearly 8 feet, are among the largest snakes of the south Indian mountains and also range from Afghanistan to China and Java. Very effective rodent-hunters, they hunt by day and chase their prey even into the forest canopy.

Although the Dhaman is supposed to be one of the favorite prey species of the King Cobra in these mountains, amusingly enough, they are assumed by local people to be the male of the King Cobra.

When disturbed or picked up, these large, greenish-brown snakes produce a curious roaring noise in their throat, the mechanism of which is not yet understood.

Egg-eating Snake

Dasypeltis scabra

Some snakes have specialized for a single food source; examples are the six species of African egg-eating snakes. From hatchlings to adults, in all stages of their life, they eat only bird eggs, swallowing them whole, crushing them in their throat, and regurgitating the shell after squeezing out the nutrients. A complex rebuilding of their skull and the development of suction ridges instead of teeth allow them to stretch their jaws over eggs that have three to four times the diameter of their body. The egg's shell is ruptured by spines, projecting from their backbone, which lie bare in the throat like posterior teeth.

The Blotched Egg-eater, which measures from 24 to 30 inches, is the most common species, ranging over most of Africa from Arabia to the Cape. In much of the range, the harmless egg-eaters are protected by imitating the color and behavior of some small African vipers.

African Slug-eating Snake
Duberria lutrix

These small snakes represent a parallel to the red-bellied snakes of North America in feeding extensively upon soft-bodied slugs and similar prey items. The 6- to 12-inch snakes are often very common although not obvious. Several species range very widely across the continent of Africa. These slug-eaters seem to recognize their prey by smell mediated by the tongue. During the day they may follow the movements of their prey by sight as well. During attack, the snake gapes widely and strikes the extended slug at midbody; it moves its jaws quickly over the prey and thus neutralizes the slug's capacity to produce sticky slime.

Sri Lankan Ground Snake

Aspidura trachyprocta

Four species of these diminutive fossorial (hiding) snakes have been described from the island of Sri Lanka. While they have a more or less conical head, they are higher snakes (colubrids) and not related to the uropeltids also found on that island. The body is stout, the tail short and pointed, and the color shows amazing variability ranging from bright reds to dark browns and black, often in the same locality. Similarly the ventral surface may be clear or marbled.

These small snakes, rarely exceeding 12 inches in length, lay their eggs in cavities 6 to 12 inches deep within the soil. Ground snakes are common in marshy areas and in irrigated agricultural regions. They may be enormously abundant in some tea plantations where they must represent an important control agent for invertebrate pests. These snakes are often found in the same place and seem to feed on the same worms as *Rhinophis,* but these two seem to be immune to each other's parasites.

South American Snail-eating Snake

Dipsas indica

These nocturnal, arboreal snakes feed mainly on living snails, which they extract from the shell. To do so the snake follows the living snail and grabs its soft body close to the shell. As the snail retracts, it pulls the snake's lower jaw into the shell. The tooth-bearing bones of the snake's upper jaw simultaneously bend inward so that they can slide over the shell without breaking it. The snake then withdraws one mandible at a time, stretching the snail's body further with each movement until the connection to the shell breaks and the soft tissues can be swallowed without the shell.

There are many species of South American snail-eaters, almost all less than 3 feet in length, each specializing for a few types of snails and hunting for these in the tropical rain forests.

Rainbow Snake

Abastor erythrogrammus

Two 4-foot-long, smooth-scaled, semi-burrowing, aquatic snakes, the Rainbow Snake and the Mud Snake, range across the moist subtropical regions of the United States extending north to Maryland and west to eastern Texas.

Both species feed on invertebrates, salamanders, fishes, and frogs which they swallow alive and then suffocate. For its food source the Mud Snake specializes in the large, elongate, aquatic salamanders, such as the Congo eel, commonly found in Florida and along the Gulf coastal regions. They can constrict, but often do not do so.

Both the Rainbow and the Mud Snakes are very brightly colored and show the shiny iridescence in their very smooth scales.

Eastern Hog-nosed Snake

Heterodon platyrhinos

The hog-nosed snakes are one of several groups of snakes that have transformed the edge of their upper jaw into hardened ridges that meet in an upturned crest at the tip of the snout. All such snakes feed almost exclusively on toads and use this pointed ridge and sharp, long teeth to penetrate the sides of their prey. This specialization compensates for the toad's tendency to inflate itself when attacked: puncturing the "balloon" makes the prey easier to swallow. The snakes also seem to have a detoxifying system allowing them to eat these rather poisonous amphibians.

When disturbed, the hog-nosed snake inflates itself or flattens its body; it then hisses, which leads to the erroneous popular name of "spreading adder." Should this behavior not deter the disturber, the hog-nosed snake will continue the bluff by rolling over onto its back, displaying the whitish belly scales. When such a "death-feigning" snake is righted, it immediately rolls back into the "proper" position of a dead snake.

The Eastern Hog-nosed Snake, up to 4 feet long, is found in the eastern and central United States west to South Dakota and Texas.

Common Water Snake

Natrix sipedon

A series of water snakes ranges over the North American continent, with some close relatives occurring in Europe. These reptiles frequent the edges of rivers, ponds, and streams, are effective swimmers that forage along the bottom of water courses, and, in some cases, even enter brackish waters along the Atlantic coastal marshes.

All water snakes have keeled scales, and the American species give birth to live young. While they are sometimes mistaken for Water Moccasins, the shape of the head proves characteristic: the true Moccasin (page 149) shows a flat head coming to a sharp edge around the front while the head of the harmless water snake is rounded. These snakes may be as large as 4 feet in length, but the average size is less than 3 feet long.

Water snakes feed on various aquatic animals; one species specializes in crayfish.

▲ Eastern Hog-nosed Snake ▼ Feigning death

▼ Common Water Snake

Red-bellied Snake

Storeria occipitomaculata

Many parts of the world harbor numerous small snakes that have specialized for one or another limited food source. Many such snakes, such as the Red-bellied Snake of the northeastern United States, are common though not usually noticed. The Red-bellied Snake is less than a foot long, gives birth to from ten to 20 live young during the summer, and may be generally recognized by a dark-brown to blackish dorsal color and a bright-red belly.

While it will also take other invertebrates, the Red-bellied Snake has specialized for feeding on slugs. When about to feed, the snake curls its lips out and up, as if it were sneering. It then bites the slug and very rapidly pulls it into its mouth by action of the upper and lower tooth rows. The process proceeds very quickly in order to limit time for the slug to produce mucus and thereby prevent the labial scales, which remain curled out of the way, from becoming fouled.

Common Garter Snake

Thamnophis sirtalis

This is by far the most common of the ribbon and garter snakes; it ranges from Texas to Alaska and from California to New England. Altogether there are more than a dozen species of snakes in this genus and nine varieties of the Common Garter Snake. The garter snake, particularly in the northeastern states, may occur in enormous numbers, and great aggregations may be seen along stream courses during hibernation.

While these animals are closely related to the water snakes, they are generally more slender, feed on smaller prey such as earthworms, invertebrates, minnows, and small frogs, and range farther away from water.

Most commonly these snakes, which attain lengths of between 20 and 40 inches, show various kinds of brownish and yellowish stripes along the back as well as some checkerboard or blotched pattern superimposed on these.

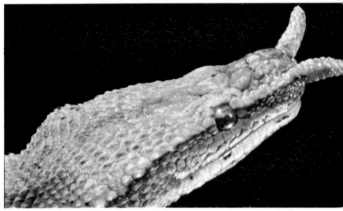

Tentacled False Water Snake

Erpeton tentaculatum

This is probably the most bizarre member of the false water snakes or homalopsines of east Asia. All of these rear-fanged snakes appear to have specialized for life in the swamps and coastal river courses of the Indo-Malaysian region. Different species feed on frogs, fishes, and such aquatic invertebrates as crabs, for which their venom is specific.

The small species, generally less than 3 feet in length, reach their peak of curious specialization in the 2-foot-long Tentacled Snake which sports two scale-covered flaps of skin, projecting from its nose (hence the name). Unfortunately, we do not know anything about the function of these tentacles: laboratory and field observations on how the animals use them are lacking.

Mangrove Snake
Boiga dendrophila

This showy snake of the moist lowland forests of eastern Asia is one of the larger rear-fanged snakes, adults reaching 8 feet in length. As in other such species, one or two teeth at the back of the upper jaw have become enlarged and sometimes grooved. The simple duct of a venom gland pours poison into the tissues at the base of the fang.

Except for the largest rear-fanged snakes, these animals are not dangerous to man, but the poison is highly specific for their prey, whether crayfish or crab, fish or lizard, frog or bird. Mangrove Snakes can be poisonous to man, but their large size, beautiful coloration, and calm temper have made these arboreal snakes favored exhibit animals in many zoos.

Scarlet Snake

Cemophora coccinea

The small Scarlet Snakes of the northeastern United States are extremely pretty animals with their red blotches bordered with black on a cream background. From 8 to 24 inches long, they are subterranean, egg-laying animals that feed mostly on small vertebrates. Some people have commented on the resemblance of this snake to the poisonous coral snake with the suggestion that it may derive some protection by imitating the color pattern of the poisonous snake. However, their ranges overlap only slightly.

During certain seasons of the year the Scarlet Snake adapts to an unusual food source—the eggs of turtles. Scarlet Snakes can sniff out turtle nests and dig their way into them; if the eggs are still fresh they use the posterior, scimitar-like tooth of the upper jaw to rip a slit. They then immerse their head into the egg and drink the liquid.

Flying Snake

Chrysopelea paradisi

Some half-dozen snakes of this beautiful arboreal genus are found in various parts of the Indo-Malaysian tropics. All are excellent climbers and show various color patterns with the scales of the back, often jet-black, setting off spots or margins of light or saturated green and yellow.

While there is some question about the classification of the group, it is clear that at least two of the species are excellent gliders. They launch themselves into the air, keeping their body in an S-shaped curve and steering with the tail. Apparently the belly scales are flattened or hollowed and produce a parachuting effect, slowing down the fall and causing the snake to glide sideways in a well-controlled fall.

About 3 feet long, these snakes feed on small lizards.

Blunt-headed Tree Snake

Imantodes cenchoa

These small tree snakes of Central and South America, with their large heads and truly slender bodies, are the peak acrobats among snakes. Apparently they sleep coiled in branches of bushes and trees and only rarely descend to the ground. They can stretch out more than two-thirds of their 2- to 3-foot-long body in a straight line to another branch while stabilizing themselves with a simple coil of the tail. They are able to cantilever the body in this way because of the slender interlocking vertebrae which are held in position by slips of longitudinal muscles paralleling the vertebral column.

They feed on lizards and some arboreal invertebrates, and their rear-fanged teeth apparently help to immobilize their prey. The advantage of this immobilization is obvious: such a slender snake could hardly have evolved if it had to struggle when feeding on bulky prey.

Vine Snake

Oxybelis fulgidus

The tropical forests of South America are the home of this Green Vine Snake, in form very similar to some unrelated species of southern Asia. All Vine Snakes tend to have pointed heads and slender bodies and may reach a length of about 4 feet. They are rear-fanged and their venom specifically paralyzes small lizards, such as the anole. When hunting or otherwise excited these snakes project the anterior tip of the tongue but, rather than flicking it as other snakes do when sampling the environment, they keep it projecting while moving along.

In passing from branch to branch the Vine Snakes move in a jerky fashion, and one can see that they increase their wavy progression whenever the wind rustles the adjoining leaves. In this way they are apparently camouflaged in behavior as well as in shape and color.

Boomslang

Dispholidus typus

This is the most advanced and most dangerous of the boigine or rear-fanged snakes. The posterior teeth are grooved and enlarged into fangs that receive very potent venom from a true venom gland. The snake is also able to rotate the tooth-bearing bone so that the fangs are brought into striking position. The venom is very effective on warm-blooded prey, and several human fatalities have been reported.

Ranging widely over the African continent, these 6-foot snakes are often mistaken for mambas but are quite dangerous in their own right. When frightened or disturbed the Boomslang inflates its neck, puffs itself out, and strikes at the intruder with open mouth.

The Boomslang is a tree snake traveling by undulation through the rough branches of thorny trees, where it normally hunts birds.

Death Adder

Acanthophis antarcticus

Though an elapid, a relative of the cobras, this brown and yellow snake looks more like a viper. Thus, the highly poisonous Death Adder has the short, stout body and triangular head often associated with vipers, yet it has well-fixed fangs in the anterior part of its mouth as do other elapids.

Though more than 60 percent of the species of Australian snakes are venomous elapids, they are not particularly common. The absolute percentage is one of those statistics that causes people to shudder, particularly people from North America, where most species and most specimens encountered are likely to be harmless. The absence of true vipers in Australia apparently allowed for specialization of some elapids, like the Death Adder, into a viper-like manner of making their living. Probably these thickset, short-bodied elapids (up to 3 feet) could not compete with more specialized vipers elsewhere.

Blue Krait

Bungarus caeruleus

This is a large snake, exceeding 6 feet in length, having a very potent neurotoxic venom. Kraits are ground snakes and vary drastically in temperament. The Blue Krait is nervous and aggressive, but the Banded Krait is a very quiet animal that, in captivity, usually will not bite. In the field, it bites only at night.

Banded Kraits will sometimes take rodents but prefer other snakes. The venom of some species contains effective nerve poisons including specific compounds that act upon the connections (motor end plates) of nerves to the muscles of the diaphragm. In the Banded Krait the venom is extremely viscous so that it apparently must be introduced into the prey by a slow chewing action, but because of its potency, not much needs to

be injected to be highly effective.

Green Mamba

Dendroaspis angusticeps

Four species of the arboreal mambas range across most of Africa. They are mainly tree and bush snakes that rest up in tree tops where they feed on birds, lizards, and arboreal rodents. They have the reputation of being fast, vindictive, and deadly. Only the last attribute is probably correct. Their speed on the ground probably does not exceed six miles per hour for a large specimen. Even if they climb somewhat more slowly than this, they do move much faster in a tree than would a man. Though relatives of the cobra, they can move their fangs forward for a bite, and their long head and large mouth insure that good contact is made with the prey.

Like numbers of several groups of snakes, the males engage in ritual combat during the mating season, rising up and intertwining their bodies, wrestling across the ground, but never biting or using their fangs. The mambas are egg-layers.

This mamba reaches a length of about 7 feet, but other species may measure more than 10 feet.

Common Coral Snake

Micrurus fulvius

The Common Coral Snake is one of two species of coral snakes occurring in the United States and of more than 40 species found in Latin America. The North American species—but not the many Latin American ones—may be recognized by the black nose. All are related to the cobras and produce very small quantities of a highly potent venom that leads to respiratory and cardiac arrest.

A whole variety of unrelated snakes, some rear-fanged and mildly poisonous and others harmless, show a similar banding in various combinations of red, white-yellow, and black. These banded snakes, averaging between 2 and 3 feet, occur throughout the Americas, where most of their small prey either avoid coral snakes altogether or treat any snake so marked with caution. Coral snakes themselves mainly live in hidden sites foraging on the forest floor or go down tunnels after burrowing lizards, small snakes, and amphisbaenians. Most bites in the United States occur when someone foolishly picks up the "pretty" snake.

Central American False Coral Snake
Rhinobothryum bovalli

In spite of more than a hundred years of exploration, we still know relatively little about many of the snakes and lizards of the Americas. Only perhaps a dozen specimens of this False Coral Snake have ever been collected in the forests of Costa Rica and Panama. While this brightly colored species resembles the general shape of the blunt-headed tree snakes it seems to be more pugnacious and will strike at a disturber.

This False Coral Snake is one of several dozen species that form a mimicry complex associated with the deadly poisonous coral snakes of the Americas. All share a pattern of banding in various combinations of black, and shadings of reds and yellows. While the patterns differ from place to place, they are strikingly similar in any locality. The assumption is that the pattern becomes "known" to potential predators and that these avoid the coral snakes as well as their mimics. Yet many of the mimics are themselves mildly poisonous and may contribute to the reinforcement of the signal in potential predators. While the system has been known for more than a hundred years, its complexities are still the subject of fruitful study today. **135**

▲ Indian Cobra ▼ Spitting Cobra ▲ Hood of Indian Cobra

Common or Indian Cobra

Naja naja

This cobra and its relatives range through the land areas of eastern Asia from Iran to China, south to Sri Lanka (Ceylon), and north to Russia. Other species of the genus occur in Africa, which is truly the home of cobras since it contains far more kinds than all of Asia.

When disturbed, they raise the anterior portion of the 6-foot body and spread some of the ribs, forming a hood. The back and front of the hood may bear different designs, such as the pair of eye spots on the back of the Indian Cobra. Since the strike is downward and forward, the height to which the hood is raised gives some indication of the distance of the strike, allowing snake charmers continuous information on how to stay out of reach. The flute often used by such performers affects the audience more than the snake, which hears well only in the low range up to 1,000 hertz.

Spitting Cobra

Naja nigricollis

A number of cobras, including this 3-foot-long true "spitter," have developed a remarkably effective way of deterring potential disturbers without getting close enough to be damaged. Each of its two hollow fangs has a small cup near the exit of the central canal so that the venom does not just pass straight out but curves, as in a turbine bucket, into an outwardly directed stream. The Spitting Cobra may open its mouth and by suddenly compressing the venom glands, send twin jets of venom toward the eyes of a cat, antelope, or man. The venom, which can be sprayed a distance of 8 feet, is absorbed through the membranes of the eye, blinding the recipient—at least temporarily.

This cobra ranges far across the African continent except in the extreme south, in some deserts, and in the deep rain forests of central and western Africa. Like the other true cobras the Spitting Cobra lays eggs. In contrast, the Ringhals, a cobra relative, produces live young. **137**

King Cobra

Ophiophagus hannah

The King Cobra is the longest of all poisonous snakes. Its skin is an olive-green base color which has a beautiful, velvety sheen in healthy specimens. King Cobras grow to be 16 feet long, but even a 12-foot specimen with the hood raised almost a yard off the ground is a spectacular sight.

King Cobras lay eggs and build nests which the mother protects by coiling about them. Before depositing the eggs the mother piles up a mound of leaves which she pulls together by sweeping coils of her body across the forest floor.

The King Cobra feeds almost exclusively on other snakes, which it catches in the forested regions of eastern Asia, where several races have been recognized.

Zookeepers report that these large snakes are quite intelligent and can be trained. Photos of Burmese priests kissing the hood of an erect cobra during ceremonies suggest some justification for this claim.

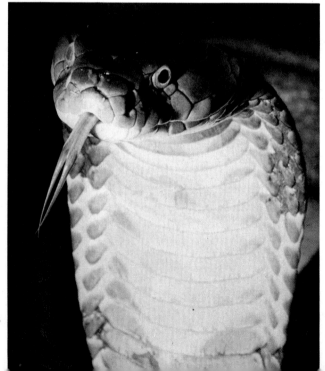

Blue-banded Sea Snake

Hydrophis cyanocinctus

Most of the poisonous sea snakes, which are relatives of the cobras, occur along the shores of southern Asia and in the Indian Ocean and the Pacific, extending west to the Gulf of Iran.

Like the cobras, they are equipped with a pair of enlarged fangs that are situated at the front of the mouth and that receive a potent venom from large glands on the sides of the head. The venom contains some unique components and apparently attacks and breaks down the muscles of the body: when mammals are bitten they often die of kidney failure.

Many of the sea snakes are characterized by a very fat, laterally flattened and ventrally keeled body and a slender neck and head. This allows them to strike to the side and catch small fishes by moving the head and neck, without moving the body. Among sea snakes, this snake represents the longest genus, with some specimens approaching 8 feet. **139**

Pelagic Sea Snake

Pelamis platurus

This striped sea snake is probably the most thoroughly oceanic of all snakes. A marvelously effective swimmer, its body has been restructured by a flattening of the tail and the formation of a ventral fold of skin, which allows it to swim like an eel. Seldom more than 3 feet in length, it is one of the smaller species of sea snakes. It gives birth to live young, which are born in the open ocean.

Although it ranges across the Pacific it apparently prefers certain areas such as the intersection of currents off Colombia and Panama where hundreds of thousands of specimens have been observed. Locomotor specialization has proceeded to the point where these snakes have trouble moving on land or returning to the water if stranded by the tide. They feed on elongate fishes which they immobilize with an injection of strong nerve poison.

Like all other snakes they periodically shed their skin which, in this case, also allows them to clean off barnacles and other invertebrates that may temporarily settle on them. Indeed, they have developed a special cleaning movement for which they twist themselves into a knot and run the whole body through it so that a coil continuously scrapes all parts.

Southern Mole Viper
Atractaspis bibronii

Most vipers are surface and tree snakes with a well-defined head that clearly seems larger than the body. In contrast, most cobras (elapids) have an inconspicuous head. The African Mole Vipers resemble elapid snakes in that the head is small and does not exceed the diameter of the body, which is 18 to 24 inches long. This clearly is an adaptation for moving about in underground tunnels where a big head might limit travel. Their trunk, which is a little heavier in the middle than at the ends, has become completely cylindrical.

These shiny, black snakes have a very potent venom that destroys the nervous system of their prey, first paralyzing and then killing. The fangs are so long that they cannot be fully erected. Rather than opening the mouth to deliver a stabbing strike, the snake slips the lower jaw to one side, exposes a fang, and hooks the prey by a backward pull against the exposed fang. The viper can thus crawl up next to a mouse or lizard and "bite" it without "opening" the mouth. Many herpetologists have discovered, to their regret, that they cannot hold these snakes behind the head without being bitten.

Gaboon Viper

Bitis gabonica

The Gaboon Viper is certainly the fattest and probably the heaviest of African poisonous snakes: specimens more than 5 feet long with a body diameter of almost 6 inches have been reported to weigh nearly 18 pounds. Vipers of this size would have fangs well over an inch long and inject something like a teaspoon of venom. While its venom is, drop for drop, much less toxic than that of many other snakes, the sheer quantity as well as the size of the teeth and the depth to which the venom is injected are likely to send the victim into shock and there are reports of death within 15 minutes.

Actually the Gaboon Viper is a most inoffensive forest snake. Its beautiful camouflage hides it among leaf litter as it waits near rodent trails for its prey, which is captured with a very quick but short sideways strike.

Gaboon Vipers give birth to more than 50 living young that are immediately able to fend for themselves.

Puff Adder

Bitis arietans

The Puff Adder is one of the largest African vipers but a little smaller than the Gaboon Viper. Some six other, mainly smaller, species of the genus occupy other portions of the continent. The Puff Adder ranges across all of Africa, from the Cape almost to the Mediterranean. Unlike the Gaboon Viper, the Puff Adder occupies subdeserts and savannas and also ascends mountain ridges.

Both of these large snakes often move by rectilinear locomotion, sliding in a straight line like a caterpillar. The highly potent venom of the Puff Adder lacks the neurological component of the venom of the Gaboon Viper: it produces severe tissue destruction.

The young are born alive in litters as large as those of the Gaboon. **143**

Saw-scaled Viper

Echis carinatus

The races of this very dangerous snake extend from Western Africa across that continent to Egypt, and east through Asia Minor, Iran, Afghanistan, Pakistan, and India to Sri Lanka (Ceylon). The various populations differ in size and behavior. The deserts of Egypt, Jordan, and Israel are inhabited by the Colored Viper, a related but more beautiful species of limited distribution. Most populations of the Saw-scaled Vipers are excellent sidewinders that are at home in deserts, where they feed on rodents and lizards.

When disturbed, this snake forms itself into an open C-shaped coil and rubs the sides of its body together bringing into contact the saw-toothed scales that give it its name. The rubbing produces a hissing sound that is amplified by the inflated body.

Although this viper rarely grows to more than 3 feet in length, it has large teeth and venom that has very high toxicity, apparently quickly dissolving the tissues, and victims report that the bite is exceedingly painful.

Common Viper

Vipera berus

This small viper ranges from Spain to the Arctic Circle (in Finland) and east through the Balkans and the Carpathians to the Caucasus. It used to be common in England and, according to legend, is one of the snakes that St. Patrick drove out of Ireland.

While local populations vary in color pattern, the central European form shows a silvery-grey back marked by a wide, blackish-brown line in a zigzag pattern. These small (2-foot-long), live-bearing snakes are vipers, characterized by having their fangs located on a movable bone. The fangs, which are folded back against the roof of the mouth when the jaws are closed, can be erected for stabbing into prey when the mouth is open.

Some half-dozen other species, partly overlapping the range of this viper, belong in the same genus, which also includes Russell's Viper.

Russell's Viper or Daboya

Vipera russelli

Russell's Viper, or Daboya, is a large, beautiful, and deadly snake, the Tic polonga of the Indies. The species' range is from India to Indonesia. It has a highly potent, mainly tissue-destroying venom, which often acts quite slowly but progressively, and which also shows strong inhibition of blood coagulation.

Russell's Vipers are easily recognized by the discrete brownish blotches on the back, each of which contains a hollow center outlined by a black line. When disturbed these snakes produce a very deep, penetrating, and protracted hissing sound. The snake, which may reach a length of 5 feet, gives birth to up to 66 live young, which are born in midsummer.

The Daboya is an effective predator on rodents and has been known to enter farms and village huts in search of its prey.

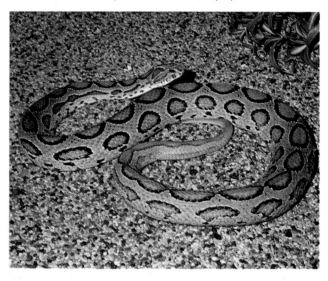

Copperhead

Agkistrodon contortrix

The Copperhead, at 16 to 36 inches, is one of the smaller North American pit vipers, a close relative of the Water Moccasin and member of the group that includes the rattlesnakes as well. All of these snakes show a deep pit about halfway between nostril and eye. The pits of the two sides contain temperature receptors allowing the snakes to range in on and aim a strike at warm-blooded animals that pass in front of them. The pits are functionally similar to, but originated independently from, the temperature sensors seen in boas and pythons.

Copperheads, which range from the eastern United States west to Texas and Missouri, also feed on frogs and lizards and have been known to take even cicadas and other insects.

It is a smaller snake than the Water Moccasin and its bite poses less danger, but both have a hemotoxic (blood-destroying) venom.

Mamushi

Agkistrodon halys

This pit viper occupies an enormous range from central Asiatic Russia into Korea and on to the Japanese islands, where it is called Mamushi. The species occurs in deserts and up to 10,000 feet into the Asian mountains.

It is a live-bearing snake, and the females have sperm storage pockets so that they may produce young as much as three years after copulation.

The Mamushi is a close relative of the Copperhead; this affinity as well as that of some other animals and plants suggests a close relationship between the organisms of eastern Asia and those of eastern North America.

Mamushi are eaten in various regions of their range, and their blood and other tissues are popularly supposed to possess healing qualities that have not yet been documented scientifically.

Water Moccasin or Cottonmouth

Agkistrodon piscivorus

This is a fairly large (6-foot) and heavy snake of the swamps and canebrakes of the southeastern United States, whence it ranges inward along the large rivers reaching as far as southern Illinois and Missouri. The Cottonmouth hibernates in the winter along the rocky ridges overlooking the rivers. Water Moccasins feed on many aquatic animals, particularly fishes. On some offshore islands in the Gulf of Mexico populations subsist under bird rookeries, eating rats and fishes brought by sea birds to feed their young and dropped by mistake.

The name Cottonmouth derives from the white lining of the mouth, which is exposed as the mouth is gaped open when the animal is disturbed.

Although the venom is highly toxic, the Cottonmouth, like many other poisonous snakes, is only slightly affected by bites from other members of the same species.

Fer-de-lance

Bothrops atrox

The Fer-de-lance is a South American pit viper. Members of this genus range from Central America far south onto the continent. This species grows to well over 7 feet long in Central America. The head of such a snake is 2½ inches long and the erectable fangs almost an inch from base to point.

These beautifully blotched snakes occupy wet forest sites and are often found floating among the mats of water hyacinths in tropical rivers. They feed on rodents and give birth to more than 60 living young. The young have a bright-yellow tail which they wave, attracting the small lizards upon which they feed.

The bite is deadly, and the venom causes severe tissue destruction that leads to rapid death unless anti-venom is available.

Mano-de-piedra

Bothrops nummifera

The Mano-de-piedra is relatively the stoutest of the large pit vipers of South America. The name comes from its resemblance to the stone implement used in crushing corn. These snakes show pattern polymorphism, some specimens being uniformly colored while others from the same litter are banded in various shades of brown.

The snake is also called "jumping viper" because of the force with which it strikes at disturbers. Reports indicate that it may actually propel itself into the air for an inch or two; certainly the strike may cause the snake to slide along the ground for a short distance, thus effectively increasing the defense radius of this short, but highly poisonous, animal, which rarely reaches 3 feet in length.

151

Diamondback Rattlesnake

Crotalus adamanteus

Sometimes attaining a length of more than 7 feet, the Diamondback Rattlesnake is the largest, heaviest, and perhaps most beautiful of the American pit vipers. It used to be very common but has become less obvious in the palmetto country of Florida and adjacent Gulf states.

These heavy snakes often move by rectilinear motion, sliding the belly skin forward and backward but keeping the body moving constantly in a straight line. They swim very well, reach many of the coastal islands, and have been found miles out to sea.

While the Diamondback feeds on various small mammals, adults feed extensively on rabbits. The fangs are proportional to the snake's length, and although the venom is not particularly potent, the amount of the dose and the depth of the bite determine its danger to man.

The rattle on the snake's tail consists of wedged caps of keratin. Each time the snake sheds its skin (sometimes four times a year), one more cap is added. When the tail is vibrated, the rattle makes a sound that may deter predators.

Sidewinder Rattlesnake

Crotalus cerastes

The Sidewinder, at 18 to 30 inches in length, is a small rattlesnake of the western United States desert that has developed a method of locomotion which involves rolling rather than undulating its body along the ground. The motion, which proceeds quickly and is difficult to understand or describe, makes use of static friction to keep the snake from slipping when it is crossing the soft sand of dunes. Sidewinders can thus travel over sand dunes faster than other snakes and move well for over a mile at a stretch.

Sidewinders are nocturnal; during the day, when the surface temperatures are much too high for any snake, they burrow in the sand under bushes. This snake uses its effective propulsion to search the desert for the small rodents and lizards which make up its food. **153**

South American Rattlesnake

Crotalus durissus

Among the more than 30 kinds of rattlesnakes, the South American species ranges from the Mexican border well down to Argentina. This 6-foot rattler shows the normal blotches along the back but has these fused into a series of stripes along the sides of the neck. These stripes are emphasized when the animal assumes its defensive coil, during which part of the body is held off the ground ready to strike.

Almost all the North American rattlesnake venoms primarily attack the cells of the blood and the lining of the blood vessels, destroying tissue. The South American Rattlesnake, in contrast, has a venom drastically different from that of most other rattlesnakes in that it contains a nerve poison that paralyzes the muscles.

Massasauga
Sistrurus catenatus

The Massasauga is one of the dwarf rattlesnakes. Unlike the true rattlesnakes, it does not have the head covered with small scales but retains the large shields also found in the Copperhead and colubrid snakes. Their rattle has been compared to the buzz of a bee.

The Massasauga is a swamp snake which has a disjunct distribution through the northeastern United States, generally occurring near bogs, where it feeds on frogs, lizards, and some rodents; occasional records also refer to invertebrate food. These 2- to 3-foot rattlers produce a relatively harmless venom, and human fatalities from their bite are rare. The young are born alive, and the litter size increases with age.

Bushmaster

Lachesis muta

The Bushmaster is the largest and certainly among the most deadly of
South American snakes. Contrary to earlier accounts, it appears to be a
rather inoffensive animal: there are now many accounts of people
having passed well within the snake's striking distance without eliciting
a visible response.

The Bushmaster grows to be 12 feet long and differs from all other
American pit vipers in that it lays eggs. Its very beautiful skin is pale
brown, often with a pinkish tone on which a series of large, dark-brown,
geometrically spaced blotches march down the back. The scales of the
Bushmaster differ from those of most other snakes: instead of being
variously flattened or keeled plates, each is rounded into a knob-like
structure that gives the snake's body a pebbled appearance.

Bushmasters are rather shy and do not survive well in captivity,
possibly because they are adapted to the relatively cool temperatures of
the heavily forested areas which never reach the high temperature levels
of open tropical savannas.

156   The specific name *muta* refers to the lack of a rattle.

Bamboo Pit Viper

Trimeresurus sp.

These green tree vipers still represent a thorough confusion since there must be more than ten kinds informally included under the single name. Two to 4 feet in length, they live in the low and highland forests of eastern Asia, are generally green, although some are brownish, show more or less patterned scales, have white, green, or red eyes, and are quite poisonous. Like other pit vipers they have erectile fangs.

Most of the green species are excellent climbers and some of them parallel similar South American animals of the genus *Bothrops* in having prehensile tails with which they hook themselves into vegetation. Since they occur in mountains up to an altitude of 9,000 feet and tend to rest in tea and cardamom bushes, they represent a high risk for the pickers.

Index

Add to your
KNOWLEDGE
THROUGH
COLOR

(All Books $1.45 Each)
(Where marked • $1.95 Each)

The opposite page lists the currently available and constantly growing books in this new paperback series. To add to your KNOWLEDGE THROUGH COLOR library simply list the titles and mail to:

BANTAM BOOKS, INC.
Dept. KTC-1
666 Fifth Avenue
New York, N.Y. 10019

Add 25¢ to your order to cover postage and handling. Send check or money order — please! We cannot be responsible for orders containing cash.

— A Free Bantam Catalog Available Upon Request —